Fat Camp Summer

Fat Camp Summer

Advice I Would Have Given My Parents

Moira Dann

SUTHERLAND HOUSE
TORONTO, 2025

Sutherland House
416 Moore Ave., Suite 304
Toronto, ON M4G 1C9

Copyright © 2025 by Moira Dann

All rights reserved, including the right to reproduce this book or portions thereof in any form whatsoever. For information on rights and permissions or to request a special discount for bulk purchases, please contact Sutherland House at sutherlandhousebooks@gmail.com.

Sutherland House and logo are registered trademarks of The Sutherland House Inc.

First edition, May 2025

If you are interested in inviting one of our authors to a live event or media appearance, please contact sranasinghe@sutherlandhousebooks.com and visit our website at sutherlandhousebooks.com for more information.

We acknowledge the support of the Government of Canada.

Manufactured in Canada
Cover designed by Jordan Lunn
Cover photo from Adobe Stock

Library and Archives Canada Cataloguing in Publication
Title: Fat camp summer : advice I would have given my parents / Moira Dann.
Names: Dann, Moira, 1957- author
Identifiers: Canadiana (print) 2025017961X | Canadiana (ebook) 20250180103 | ISBN 9781998365005 (softcover) | ISBN 9781998365012 (EPUB)
Subjects: LCSH: Dann, Moira, 1957-—Childhood and youth. | LCSH: Camps for overweight children. | LCSH: Body image in children. | LCSH: Overweight children—Psychology. | LCSH: Obesity in children. | LCSH: Obesity—Psychological aspects. | LCSH: Parents of overweight children. | LCGFT: Autobiographies.
Classification: LCC BF723.B6 M36 2025 | DDC 306.4/613—dc23

ISBN 978-1-998365-00-5
eBook 978-1-998365-01-2

Contents

Preface: A book I'd want to read   vii

Chapter 1   Baby fat: Houston, how do we know we have a problem?   1

Chapter 2   Before: those damn jeans (and genes)   27

Chapter 3   Blindsided   35

Chapter 4   Surrender: then what?   43

Chapter 5   Division Four bunk life: food, follies, friends, and exercise   49

Chapter 6   The scale or the guillotine: weekly weigh-in   59

Chapter 7   Adolescent cynicism: "If she mentions the goddamn edema in her leg one more time, I swear…"   67

Chapter 8   Visitors' day: please release me, redux   77

Chapter 9   Rescued: it was the best day of my life   81

Chapter 10   Weight loss today   83

Epilogue: Carry that weight   95

Acknowledgments   97

Notes   99

Preface: A book I'd want to read

"Someday we'll enjoy a bottle of wine and I'll tell you about how my parents sent me to fat camp when I was thirteen."

I threw this back over my shoulder at my friend and agent, Rob Firing, as I got off an elevator.

Rob stopped the closing door with his foot and said, "Wait. What?"

"Oh, yeah," I said, turning back toward the elevator, "it's a funny story. Worth its own bottle, and a good vintage, too. I was punted off to a camp for fat girls in the Catskills back in the seventies."

Rob looked at me, perplexed, but his face instantly conveyed a visceral understanding of everything those words meant to a thirteen-year-old girl. Any thirteen year old. Any human being, really, who's sent away from home to be "fixed."

The elevator alarm started to buzz, wanting its doors to close.

"Go, go," I said, waving. "We'll talk later."

"Yes, let's talk sooner rather than later," I heard Rob say as the elevator door closed.

* * *

In the years following my 1971 sojourn at Camp Stanley ("a non-medical slim-down camp for girls"), I had reduced a traumatic incident to an anecdote—and I resisted the trauma label for a long, long time. I regarded it as an unfortunate period in my life, which then stabilized as a funny/not-funny story, depending on my audience. I mean, I survived. And how ridiculous is the idea of a bunch of fat teenagers running around at summer camp, trying to "get skinny." It's been a comedic setup for years: fat people trying not to be.

I gave Rob the story précis the next time we talked. I told him: it's a little anecdote I dine out on; it can settle a conversation if it's simmering violently toward an argument, when talk of food and size and dieting and shape and body positivity gets too aggressive or esoteric or personal or political.

"I think it's more than an anecdote," said Rob. "I think it's a book. A memoir."

"Nah. Memoir, yuck. It's such white-bread North American privilege-whining. I mean, who cares about a fat, boo-hooing old baby boomer who's had a wonderful life when there are people hungry and suffering? Before I attempt a memoir, I would have to get closer to the end of what I hope would be my long and fruitful life, loaded with accomplishment and philanthropic excesses."

When I did my MFA in creative nonfiction at University of King's College in my fifties, I had younger classmates who told me they were writing a memoir. I had to smile and bite my tongue until I tasted blood so that I wouldn't say: "A memoir!? You're not old enough to write a memoir, you're a punk, you haven't really lived!" Instead, I'd feel slimy saying: "Really? That's nice."

What I learned at King's was that my limited, old-fashioned definition of "memoir" didn't cut it anymore. My younger friends were writing memoirs, or varying-length experiential narratives, of life-changing events or intense experiences, and then extrapolating what they had learned to a broader swath of life, a bigger context, to great effect.

"I think your story could help people," said Rob.

Zing.

That was how Rob finally persuaded me to write about Camp Stanley: *This story could help people.* Maybe those who endured a similar fat-camp experience, or family isolation as "the fat one." Or people in a situation where it seemed any family difficulties couldn't be solved at home with love and common sense and maybe a counselor—so they were sent away.

It took quite a bit of back-and-forth for me to finally see it might be worth doing. Who cares if I was a chubby teen? Who cares if being sent to fat camp made me feel as though I weren't acceptable, lovable, good enough, that in fact I needed to be fixed? Who cares if the experience has marked most every decision I've made since? Who cares about my fear and shame and upset?

I stopped the stream of excuses and thought about how the fear and shame and upset are all the same, no matter what caused them.

One friend asked: how are you going to cope when you find yourself re-traumatized by writing about the event?

Initially I thought: re-traumatized? Moi? Can't happen, I've spent years in therapy and have dealt with everything. It's all good. No worries. No problem. Nuh-uh, not me.

And then I looked at how I felt and how I was avoiding writing about the near-fist fight my mother and I had. I noted how I was having nightmares and sleep difficulties. The physical feelings, echoes of those attached to ancient anxiety and paranoia I experienced.

When I thought about how, actively and passively, I'd sought out stories like mine over the years, looking for support and solace; stories that weren't laugh-at-the-fat-kid tales of torment, or long-form narratives or journal excerpts written by people who suffered much more than I did. (*An Angel at My Table* by Janet Frame comes to mind; it is one of many.) I thought maybe Rob is right. Maybe this could help some people feel better about themselves. Or help people who've experienced what they perceive as conditional love—pretty much all of us.

I offer this story with the hope it generates some understanding and compassion, and maybe helps someone.

Moira Dann
Victoria, BC, 2025

CHAPTER 1

Baby fat: Houston, how do we know we have a problem?

"Let's talk plainly. Your child is fat and you would like to help your child lose weight. Well, I can help you."
—*Camp Stanley founder Gussie Mason, from her 1975 book* Help Your Child Lose Weight and Keep It Off

"Ow!"

I reacted when Mrs. Kindly European Seamstress stabbed me with a straight pin while pinning a shoulder strap. She apologized profusely. My mother told me I was okay.

The skilled seamstress patted the flesh beneath my shoulder blade, looking for the right words, finally saying in strongly accented English: "She is, well, you know…"

She patted me again, looking at my mother.

My mother said, "Yes, she is well-upholstered." The two women chuckled. I didn't take offense or umbrage at the time. I did want to get out of there, probably because it was a sunny day.

This was my first inkling that I might not appear fairy-sylph-like in my delicious green costume with the purple flowers and sequins at the school dance recital. I quickly forgot it, for hadn't I been selected for a short star turn at the start of a new sequence?

No, I forgot about the "well-upholstered" line while busy imagining myself in pointe shoes, leading a line of tiny dancers across the stage. That's how my mind transformed the reality of me in my pink ballet slippers struggling daintily, galumphing along to plinka-plinka piano music with a bunch of other seven year olds who participated in Saturday morning ballet classes in the assembly hall/gym at the girls' school.

I didn't think about my size too much, but I was probably in my last few cute-fat days—if I was fat at all. Six years later, when I was almost fourteen, my parents sent me to "fat camp." The many things that contributed to that decision probably started to accumulate around the time of the dance recital, before my grandmother died.

* * *

No correspondence survived that fat-camp period, and only a few Polaroids. But I hit pay dirt one day in a second-hand store, primo source documentation in book form: *Help Your Child Lose Weight and Keep it Off* by Gussie Mason. This contained the philosophy, mindset, and counsel of the woman behind Camp Stanley (and the nearby boys' equivalent, Camp Tahoe).

"Now, you can help your son or daughter become a slim, confident and happy child," reads the back-cover blurb of the book, published by Grosset and Dunlap in 1975; the paperback sold for $1.95.

Being able to consult this book meant I didn't have to rely too much on memories, even Technicolor memories, the unforgettable ones associated with varying levels of trauma; these memories can also grow fragile with age. I also didn't want to speculate too much on Mason's motivations, because my child mind had turned her into an enemy—without knowing the whole story.

I had read the book decades ago, when it first came out. In re-reading it, I surprisingly agreed with Mason on several points, while at the same time regarded many of her "Ten Commandments for Parents of Overweight Children" as largely wrong.

In her opening chapter, Mason tried to nail down the reasons there were children who needed to go to her camps.

She asked several questions, the first one being: "Did the baby fat never go away?" She noted how we love chubby infants with rosy cheeks and judge them to be healthy. Mason wonders if there might be a conscious or unconscious desire to keep children appearing healthy—by keeping them chubby.

"Is the household routine irregular?" Here Mason describes the activity level of many households, both then and now: "Mother is running off to a meeting. Dad is working late at the office, sister has been talking to her boyfriend since three in the afternoon, brother is at football practice. Somehow, in the midst of all these activities, the fat child is supposed to not only make sure he gets fed—or more often, feed himself—but also to keep track of his diet.

"On an eat-and-run schedule, it's almost impossible for a mature adult to control his weight. It *is* an impossible job to ask a child to do."

This still feels true to me; it was certainly part of my weight challenge growing up, and my health and weight difficulties as a driven, workaholic adult.

I always pegged the start of my truly overweight childhood years to my grandmother's death when I was eight years old. She lived with us and ran the household. I had a brother and a sister, and my parents both worked: my Dad in business and my Mum a teacher. I had a great relationship with my "Gammy" and she fed me well—critically, I realize now, on a schedule. She taught me how to cook and bake, maneuvering my "play'" table into a corner of the kitchen, giving me dough she'd already made and a kid-sized rolling pin. My initial baking experiments featured pie with crusts gray from my overhandling and mystery fillings. These offerings were spirited away while they "cooled" for an extended period of time, so that I never sickened anyone.

She squeezed me fresh orange juice most mornings.

Gammy died the autumn I was in third grade. I was devastated. In her absence, every day after school I made myself a cup of tea (as she would have) and then prepared a small plateful of Premium Plus salted crackers smeared with butter and jam, which I ate while seated in "her" chair. I had favorite shows on both French and English channels (*Thierry la Fronde* and *Magic Tom*). But without my grandmother's company with which to wind down my school day, the shows became my friends, which wasn't necessarily healthy.

When my grandmother was alive, I felt fine about going out after school to Brownies, or the library, or to play with my friends. After her death, for quite a while I felt too anxious to leave the house. Nothing would have appeared awry, as by the time my siblings and my mother drifted in from school in the late afternoon, my ritual was done. I just filled up on tea and crackers, unchecked by my grandmother who would have scolded me for ruining my appetite.

Gussie Mason's next question: "Does your child come from a fat environment?" She notes less than "ten percent of children of normal-weight parents are fat. When one parent is fat, the chances are two in five that they will have fat children."

A more recent study at the University of California at San Francisco is brutally frank: "A child with one obese parent has a fifty percent chance of being obese. When both parents are obese, their children have an eighty percent chance of obesity."

The measurable degree has changed over time, but the truth elicited by Mason's question remains the same: "If overweight parents want to help their overweight child to reduce, they must be ready to change some of their eating habits, too."

My mother and brother were slender. My father, a boxer in his youth, could gain weight quickly if he stopped eating well and exercising. If he got too heavy, he could just give his head a metaphorical shake and start jogging regularly. His little calorie-counting booklet would reappear. He would start refusing bread and having yogurt with maple syrup for dessert. He could be an ascetic when losing weight, but our father gave us all a palate for fine dining.

My sister and I are built like him. She is athletic: a swimmer, dancer, runner, and figure skater. My sister, slender and beautiful, dieted in her later teenage years. I never thought of her as fat. She was gorgeous and I wanted to be just like her. I am like her in at least one way: we both have a weakness for potato chips.

From her, I learned about taking a small Unico tin of tuna for lunch, and brightening it up with a squeeze of lemon. In Mason's book, she said this about tuna: "Many children have been raised to eat meat and ignore fish. But most youngsters don't consider tuna to be fish—after all, it doesn't look or smell like fish, and it comes in a can".

Mason then asks: "Did your child learn bad eating habits at an early age?" She then suggests that *mothers* who cook and feed their families food that culturally represents the family are to blame. Mason mentions "the Jewish mother who prepares knishes and blintzes" and the "Italian mother who weighs down the table with big plates of pasta," claiming both "are unconsciously teaching their children to be fat." She walks it back a bit by saying families don't need to abandon their culinary culture, "but *mothers* [my emphasis] have to be willing to learn new ways to cook traditional dishes if they want to help slim down their children."

Camp Stanley often cited its inclusion in a 1969 National Film Board of Canada film by William Weintraub, titled *A Matter of Fat*, narrated by Lorne Greene (best known as Pa Cartwright from *Bonanza*).

In it, Mason continues to lay blame: "I blame the parent, I blame the mother; I can't blame the father because the father is not home, he's out earning the money that the mother is spending to make this child fat."

My household suffered more from the busy-life blues than from any great culinary cultural imperative, beyond a love of good food.

We had a ritual evening Sunday dinner, a roast of beef or chicken. Every Friday we ordered out, sometimes Chinese-Canadian food (I loved chicken soo guy, with the breading and the sweet sauce) but usually BBQ chicken with sauce, cole slaw, and french fries. We'd sit in the living room where I had the pleated aluminum dish on a tray on my knees, eating and watching *The Time Tunnel* or *The Man from U.N.C.L.E.*

This continued later on, when I was a teenager and the only child still at home. My mother would offer to order from St-Hubert BBQ, a quarter-chicken dinner with sauce, fries, and coleslaw. Sometimes I sang the jingle as a lobbying tactic: "Ding-a-ling-a-ling/que desirez-vous/puth-puth-puth/ St. Hubert bar-be-cue!" Sometimes, at my request, a slice of Black Forest cake was added to the order.

This was post-Camp Stanley, when I was thin, and struggling to stay that way. After years of night school, my mother had gone back to college full-time to get her BA. My father was always busy, although never too busy to check in on my mental health periodically. "How's your morale these days?" he'd say.

I mention this because I don't like to see mothers take all the blame for fat kids. As I've traipsed, exhausted, through much of my adult life, it's made me more sympathetic toward my mother, doing all she did for so long: teaching school, going to school, being a wife, a mother, a daughter, a friend, a world citizen. I wish our household nutrition had been better, but my mother was under a great deal of pressure, including pressure from the growing food industry. My head was easily turned: I remember lobbying for breakfast Tang (what the astronauts drank) over fresh-squeezed orange juice.

My grandmother's menus, on the other hand, were old-fashioned: meatloaf, stew, Western omelets (which she called "cowboy"), roasts of beef and chicken, apple pie—consistent, and on-schedule. The takeout phase only happened after she died.

Mason's query list also asks: "Has the home life changed dramatically?" She cites the regular moves of military families that can lead to childhood upset and less physical activity. My home life changed dramatically following the loss of my grandmother. She had been my primary adult. I was sad that more family members weren't as sad as I was about her loss. I didn't know whom to ask about this, as it was the kind of question I would normally have asked Gammy.

Years later, I asked my mother about how expressions of grief seemed to shut down right after the funeral; she said she was very sad after her mother died, but didn't want to upset the kids—so she kept it to herself. That's what I did, too, I told her. I couldn't see anywhere to let it out. I wrote letters and cards to my grandmother and "mailed" them to her by throwing them up to the top shelf in the dining room closet, the spot in the house my eight-year-old mind thought was closest to heaven.

* * *

Mason's penultimate question is this: "Is your child using food as a weapon?" She expands by suggesting that a girl with a beautiful mother might eat too much and gain weight "because that is the best way to avoid competition." A boy might do the same to avoid comparisons with an athletic father.

Mason acknowledges a child probably isn't doing this consciously, but recommends parents consider their child's situations, their comments, and their actions to get an idea "of whether or not your child is punishing you by getting fat."

This idea is pretty much non-existent today, where obesity is sometimes equated with child abuse. Experts as well as other parents wonder if parents of an obese child should be shunned, fined, or, at the very least, blamed.

Parent-blaming is not useful, as a general rule. Even Mason recognizes that weight control is best regarded as "a family project." She even put that in her "commandments" for parents.

However, the idea of a child trying to leverage his or her obesity is still worth examining. If a child's weight really, really bothers a status-conscious parent, I can understand how a child might enjoy being a mosquito-like irritant, particularly if there are plans afoot to change the child. I sometimes enjoyed annoying my mother, the English teacher, with bad grammar, misusing the word "nauseous" when I meant "nauseated." Her jaw would visibly tighten, but only rarely did she correct me after the first time.

Finally, Mason asks, "Is your child driven by unconscious fears?" This is an astute question, as it addresses the twin challenges of young dieters' self-sabotage, and/or using obesity to inappropriately nurture their inner introvert. Fear of success, fear of failure: it doesn't matter which. The child or teenager who just wants to stay home, eat potato chips, read comics, or watch videos or play video games; or the teenager who has no interest in making new friends or joining a team to get some exercise.

Mason mentions the children at her camps who do everything they can to keep from losing weight. She says she has "come to the conclusion that to some children, subconsciously, being fat is a great advantage. The bigger body makes them seem stronger than they really are." They don't have to compete, worry about social invitations, or being bothered too much by other people.

I agree. Looking back, I know I enjoyed my intermittent heft because nobody messed with me. It made me feel safer. I took care never to be on my back foot and, mentally, kept my dukes up.

But other times, my heft made me miserable. I had lots of male friends, but never a boyfriend in the same city. I was great at crushing out on unattainable fellows who lived at a distance. Lots of old-fashioned love-letter romances, where I could write the perfect smart, clever version of me on narrow-rule legal pads and dot my I's with circles.

And I was no threat to my girlfriends: I didn't borrow clothes and I didn't steal boyfriends. I was the perfect sidekick.

Just as I had trouble differentiating fatigue and hunger, I couldn't discern the difference between size and strength. What I wanted was to be strong. I did figure that out in my twenties, thanks to weight training with my father, a bit before lady weightlifters were cool.

* * *

I wonder why Gussie Mason's program had to be executed in a camp environment. It might have been more effective in small groups through various community centers. Day camps. Girls could have been together during the day, taking part in physical activities with controlled meals, and could have taken all they learned home with them at night.

Camp Stanley wasn't my first camp experience, and that might have contributed to my reticence to attend. I had been to Girl Guide camp a few times, with varying results.

My first was for a weekend "pioneer camp." I lobbied for this because I wanted to be with older girls, because I wanted to be older. The older I was, the sooner I could leave home. I always felt older, an old soul waiting for inner and outer realities to synch up. They finally did around age thirty-five.

My dad helped me pack for pioneer camp, binding a tarp and a deflated air mattress and a sleeping bag in a bundle tied up with pink clothesline cord that extended to a kind of shoulder strap. That and my gear in a well-used rucksack were all I needed.

Campers arrived at the site at the edge of twilight, walking downhill in the dark with our flashlights. I could hear water burbling, so there was moving water nearby. I wasn't much help pitching a tent. I slept with other girls on lumpy ground—I couldn't get it together to pump up my air mattress. I had trouble getting to sleep and staying asleep, because my excitement/fear meant I had to pee. The grass en route to the outhouse was wet, so I had to put my white rainboots on to make the trek. The moonlight was almost enough to preclude the need for the flashlight. My bladder didn't calm down as the night went on, so I was up and down. I finally gave up taking the rainboots off and just shoved my whole self into my sleeping bag. I had also heard "something" on one of my outhouse treks, so I was getting into my sleeping bag fast to escape the nameless dread.

I must have slept but I was exhausted most of the next day, even when I was charged with getting breakfast made for our patrol. I couldn't get the fire started. Dang, I *couldn't* get the fire started. Bark firestarter, kindling twigs, small split logs—I couldn't get the fire started. Breath, to provide oxygen to the spark—I couldn't get the fire started. Others in my patrol had lots of advice but offered no help. I was almost in tears. The other patrols had finished breakfast and cleaned up.

A Girl Guide leader strode over to our campsite and authoritatively piled bark, twigs, logs—and lit it with a Zippo fished out of a deep pocket in her jeans. In a tone of I'm-not-mad-let's-just-get-on-with-it, she directed some patrol members to melt some butter in a pan over the growing flame, others to scramble eggs in the pan with a fork, others to get the bread ready on a stick to toast over the fire, and others to be ready with plates. Under adult direction, we all had barely scrambled eggs and charred bread within fifteen minutes, so we were able start our projects for the day.

Needily seeking approval, I asked my patrol leader what she had thought about breakfast. "Well, the eggs were kind of raw," she replied honestly. I was crushed, but this far from home and among strangers was no time to feel sorry for myself. Cheeks burning, it was on to the next: my camping project—a tripod washstand.

As the sun warmed, evaporating the dew, I started to relax, hear the birdsong, and enjoy being out in the country. It was too early to swim, but we dipped our feet in the freezing stream to enjoy the cold. On a hike we saw the budding trees and other emerging spring life. Subsequent meals were better orchestrated to feed us all and cooked on a bigger, communal fire built in a three-sided brick container.

This trip wasn't affected by any feelings of being fat. Sometimes in life, I felt lumpy and not lithe, struggling to function in the world where I didn't feel as though I belonged. There hadn't been anything I felt compelled to avoid, the way I avoided sports.

I left pioneer camp reasonably happy, and while eager to go home, I was also keen go to a longer sleepaway experience that summer at Camp Wa-Thik-Ane in Morin Heights, Quebec, in the Laurentian mountains.

I had been entranced by my sister's tales of going to Wa-Thik-Ane; I had romanticized them and I wanted to go, too.

I lobbied again to be in a tent with older girls. I was always concerned about getting my period around the wrong people and facing any kind of interrogation that might cause me to inadvertently break my promise to my mother not to repeat what she told me about periods, reproduction, and sex—all stuff I was dying to talk about. This I'll-be-okay-with-the-older-girls MO sometimes backfired when I heard stuff I didn't understand ("He might get you naked but that doesn't mean he'll get you pregnant") and I had no one with whom to check it.

One of the girls in my tent, after lights out, asked us all to train our flashlights on her as though they were spotlights while she did a dance. This girl was several grades ahead of me in school; I didn't really know her. What she actually did was a striptease to no music, but she did keep up a running commentary on body parts, hers and those belonging to others. I was startled, still being kind of modest, as well as curious and confused. Was this a regular thing, was it happening in all the other tents? Were we all expected to do this? I hoped not and then set to figuring out how I could decline, if asked. I could use my period as an excuse, whether I was having one or not. Would that break my promise to my mother? There were no other sexual overtures from anyone at Girl Guide camp, or experiences with sexual overtones, other than some of the frank talk from some of the girls who clearly had older brothers with porn collections. I wonder how many knew what they were really saying. Or maybe I'm a retro-Pollyanna.

We slept under canvas on raised wood-slat platforms up a short flight of wide stairs. The latrines were a walk away, as was the mess tent, which was an open-sided building with a roof.

The latrines were mighty fragrant. One camp counselor made daily rounds to pour lye down the hole; she wore rubber gloves and carried a large plastic lidded container and a smaller open one.

My tentmates liked to rewrite lyrics to some of the campfire songs, making them naughty with double-entendres or replacing lyrics with rhyming words that described rude bits. We lampooned the old-fashioned songs we sang at night while roasting marshmallows around the campfire. They would still be singing their versions after lights-out until they were convulsed with laughter or told to shut up by a patrolling counselor.

One particular favorite was an old-timey song, "My Old Flivver." It was a love song to an ancient jalopy, ending with "Bump jiggly bump bump, peep peep." It's not hard to see how it was destined to end.

It was all fun and games until the late-days decision to leave our mark in the latrine by inscribing the walls with witty bon mots—and then go swimming.

I drew a Kilroy-was-here cartoon, unsigned, and that was it. I wanted out of that latrine! Others hung around and created masterworks of sorts. I went swimming.

We were back in our tent changing when we received a summons from the Girl Guide leader. Only when we arrived at the mess tent did it occur to me that we might be in trouble for our Banksy action. The leader looked at us, stone-faced, until we were all assembled. She then motioned us to follow her and silently led the way to the latrine.

She opened the door, stepped in and pointed to the "My Old Flivver" parody: "I want the girl who did this to own up."

There were three Mississippi breaths of terrified silence before my tentmate slowly put her hand up.

I simultaneously felt relief that it wasn't my Kilroy-was-here that had been tapped, while I burned with shame for my tentmate, and felt

I had completely let down and disappointed Guides founders Lord and Lady Baden-Powell.

Our punishment was to scrub it all off the walls of the latrine. When we finished hours later, we had scrubbed our knuckles raw and reeked of bleach, which made other campers give us a wide berth as we headed to dinner.

Camp Wa-Thik-Ane wasn't a true pioneer camp but it was pretty essential. We washed our own dishes after we ate and put them in our individual plastic "dish bag" (like a string bag) that was hung on a nail, where they would dry. Before that, though, we would submerge and pull the dish-filled bag through an oblong-with-rounded edges tin bath filled with boiling water, to "disinfect" the dishes. A few times this ritual exposed our poor dishwashing technique with a sheen of oil atop the boiling bath, and we would be sent to redo the entire ritual until the boiling water ran clean.

The campsites bore names such as Algonquin and Huron and Iroquois, a rudimentary acknowledgment of where we were, who preceded us, and why we were there. We learned pathfinding techniques, semaphore, how to chop wood, start fires, cook outdoors, swim, canoe, kayak, braid plastic into friendship bracelets, tie knots, and tried to pretend we weren't just a few hours away from a major North American city.

* * *

It was doubly hard to pretend we were far away from civilization on July 16, 1969, when Apollo 11 launched. We had known before we left home it was going to happen because it was all over the news, but we had minimal outside influences when at Wa-Thik-Ane. The day Neil Armstrong landed on the moon, all pretense of being somewhere remote was shelved when we were called down to the mess hall. I wonder how it had been decided that this moment was sufficiently momentous that this group of camping girls should stay up late and watch the moon landing on a tiny black-and-white television with bad reception.

The nighttime summer sky in Morin Heights was striking. I looked up at the sky as we walked from our tent down the well-worn dirt path to the mess hall, thinking *That's the same moon shining on my house in Montreal, the same one my family might be looking at right now.* That thought had the power to make me feel either less lonely or more lonely, wherever I was.

I knew that landing on the moon was a big deal. I wondered what the planet Earth looked like from the moon. What were the astronauts seeing? Listening to the scratchy audio, and not really knowing what we were seeing in the B&W images, was still oddly moving. And it meant we got to stay up late, wrapped in blankets and drinking camp cocoa, and watch the whole thing in this strangely asynchronous situation, young girls witnessing history being made, watching space from a campsite in the woods.

I later had a photo of Earth from space on my bedroom wall, and I went to see "moon rocks" on display in the mid-seventies at the repurposed Expo '67 site. I could quote Neil Armstrong about giant steps for mankind but preferred the Buzz Aldrin line: "Neil Armstrong was the first man to walk on the moon. I am the first man to piss his pants on the moon." That line just creased me, and turned Buzz Aldrin into my favorite astronaut.

Maybe it was Apollo 11 that allowed me to be seduced by Tang, leading me to prefer it over fresh orange juice. A drink for astronauts trumped my grandmother's care.

I wasn't always hungry at Girl Guide camp. I liked the camp food at Wa-Thik-Ane. Oatmeal or scrambled eggs and toast and skim-milk cocoa. Soup and big sandwiches. Stew. While I like cocoa, I missed my tea.

For a long time, my memories of Wa-Thik-Ane were attached to something that now makes me ashamed: signatures on a piece of birch bark I peeled from a tree, although I've learned that it's okay to take it when it comes away easily from the tree early in the season.

I remember taking the bark around and getting pals to sign it, and then putting on the wall above my cupboard door.

I went to Wa-Thik-Ane one more time, a less memorable weeklong trip although I was chewed up by mosquitoes and was quite desperate to get home. That would have been 1970.

* * *

The return to school in September 1970 was more difficult. I didn't have to wear my uniform on the first day. I felt quite svelte in a grey wool skirt with a front pleat and yellow topstitching. It was quite short and I felt good in it. I wore it with knee socks and navy-blue Oxford-style shoes with a bit of a heel; we called them nun-shoes. I felt "fair grand" (my mother's term for that ineffable confident feeling about how you look) on my last day not in a school uniform, not wearing a tunic.

There was lots of roiling drama at home. Conversations long into the night, tears, lots of long conversations on the phone with the family counselor.

I give my parents credit for some of the moves they made while staggering around on uneven ground, trying to stabilize the family. One was to get us all the psychological help we needed.

I was, in my mother's words, "acting out." I wasn't doing drugs (that came later) but my grades were slipping and my attitude was bad. I watched way too much TV, skipped school (tough when your mother's a teacher), and stayed up late. I didn't hand in assignments. Failed tests. I drank a bit, too, with a couple of older friends in their basement.

Partly because of all this, I was sent to a private girls' school a few weeks into eighth grade, my second year in high school (in Quebec high school runs from grade seven through grade eleven). Another reason: it was unhealthy to be a student in the same school where my mother taught. My mother told me years later that she wished she had spotted this problem earlier. She also thought about home-schooling us all, but worried about our socialization.

Montreal was roiling politically at the time, as was the whole province of Quebec; both had been for a while due to the separatist faction that wanted Quebec to secede from Canada, especially the terrorist group Front de libération du Québec (FLQ). Our generation simply got used to riots, mailbox explosions, kidnappings, the War Measures Act, soldiers in the streets, arrests, detentions.

We endured/looked forward to bomb threats called into our school, so much so that a cartoon bomb was featured on the cover of our yearbook one year.

These bomb threats usually meant the class-changing bells rang and rang and rang and we were sent to stand in the schoolyard for minutes that felt like hours, until school administration got an all-clear and we were sent back to the classroom.

I would envision how unprotected we were in the schoolyard, in the event of actual bomb carnage. Even at the outer edges of school property, we would never be more than ten or twenty yards away from the blast, which would surely make short work of a two-story postwar institutional edifice.

We weren't offered any counseling of any kind after these events, we just kind of laughed it off: "Oh yeah, another bomb threat at school today."

* * *

I was more of a square peg in eighth grade and I was chafing with boredom at school. Everything felt unsettled. Favorite rockers Jimi Hendrix and Janis Joplin died within weeks of each other. There had been discussions, parental meetings behind closed doors, tears, entreaties from me, begging just to take some time off to think. Then, on October 5, British Trade Commissioner James Cross was kidnapped by the FLQ. A few days later, on October 8, the FLQ manifesto was broadcast on CBC. On October 10, Canadian Thanksgiving weekend, Quebec cabinet minister Pierre Laporte was kidnapped by a different cell of the FLQ.

The War Measures Act was invoked October 16. The next day, Pierre Laporte was executed. His kidnappers left a communiqué at Place Des Arts to let authorities know his body would be found in a car near St-Hubert Airport. I was at Place Des Arts that night to see a ballet version of *The Who's Tommy*. Everything was calm when I entered the theater; when I came out, the place was swarming with cops and military. It was terrifying; I was so glad my dad was there to pick me up.

In the midst of this, I was in crisis and changing schools. It's fascinating how personal crisis makes any crisis—any event at all—appear in memory as though etched there.

I was sent for some psychological testing. I saw a very nice woman doctor in a hospital setting: did some drawings, answered some questions, and took what I realized halfway through was probably an IQ test.

I felt better after this afternoon, even though it wasn't clear exactly what it was supposed to achieve. It felt as though a new beginning was now possible. I slept better that night.

Our family counselor briefed me on the results at my next appointment. Test results indicated I was a little bit depressed. I asked about the IQ test. She couldn't go into too much detail, but she wanted me to know: I could belong to Mensa.

I looked that up when I got home. I was pretty smart, apparently.

My parents were circumspect about any scores that showed how smart I was. I asked my Mum about that years later. She said she and Dad knew we were smart, and *wanted* us to know we were smart, but didn't want us to broadcast numbers inappropriately. So she told me the *range* of numbers and asked me to keep them to myself, the same way she told me about sex and my period and asked for discretion with this adult information.

This was a great gift. Because as I navigated my fat-girl adolescence, I had it in my back pocket: I could join Mensa. That became a soothing thought when hassled about my weight: *I can always lose weight, but you can't gain brains. I may not be fat forever, but you'll always be stupid*. Many internal bon mots along those lines. I never said it out loud to anyone, but it made me feel much, much better.

* * *

After all the testing, there was an interview with the headmistress of a small private girls' school in Montreal, Weston School. My sister had gone to Weston in the late sixties, after illness made it difficult for her to graduate from public school in a timely manner.

The headmistress was the formidable (in the best sense of the word) Ruthmary Lewis, née Penfield. That Mrs. Lewis was the daughter of the great neurosurgeon Wilder Penfield meant little to me at age thirteen.

Her office behind the staircase in a grand old house on Ballantyne Avenue in Montreal West was both comforting and oppressive. After my Mum and I took a tour of the classrooms-in-bedrooms, I had my interview. Mum waited outside.

I was a wreck, not having slept and fully overwhelmed by too much change happening too fast. It was cold that day, and gray. I was hungry. Mrs. Lewis sat me down in one of the two chairs in front of her desk. She moved some papers and books around on the desk's surface so she could see me, all while keeping up a calm running commentary on the school building, the neighborhood in Montreal West, the nearby dairy where students went for ice cream on lunch break, the girls' schedule, and what she was reading. I think she noticed me looking at her degrees on the wall, at least one from Bryn Mawr College, and explained how she had come to attend that renowned women-focused school. She talked about the intramural structure at Weston (three houses: Austen, Bronte, and Montgomery) and about opportunities for debating and public speaking.

Mrs. Lewis was a big believer in education for young women, and she knew how to fill the air with calming words, full of information. She finally sat down and looked at me across her desk.

"Well, Moira, tell me: what is it you want?"

I stared at the ground and said: "I want to get the fuck out of high school."

I cannot believe how rude I was. I knew the f-word but rarely used it. I kept my eyes on the ground as I waited for the sharp intake of breath, for my mother to be summoned, and the sky to fall on my head before I was sent to reform school rather than this small girls' school a short bus ride from home.

The silence went on and on and when I finally raised my eyes, Mrs. Lewis just said: "Okay, let's see what we can do."

Wait, what? I was gobsmacked. She didn't give me a lecture about keeping a civil tongue in my head, respecting my elders, or tell me I should wash my mouth out with soap for using such language. I felt a bit dizzy as she stood and spoke gently about the best day for me to start, but she thought the following week would probably suit everybody, and did I agree? I nodded like a dope, wondering now if I'd actually uttered what my mother called the Supreme Dirty Word. Mrs. Lewis went on, guiding me to the door of her office; she said I didn't need to stress about getting my perfect uniform together; a blue skirt and a blue shirt would do for now.

I remained shocked into silence for the duration of our hand-shaking and leave-taking, replete with see-you-next-week and kind smiles. My mind raced throughout, as I thought for sure my rudeness would preclude my going to Weston. But no.

Getting my faux-uniform together was fraught, and I worried about feeling fat in those days leading up to the first day at Weston. The skirt was too small, because I was growing up, but the blouse fit—pulled a bit across my bust, fixable with a small gold safety pin. There was no discernable muffin top as long as I sat with good posture. I decided not to affect the school tie until I had a tunic, but I obsessed on the two decorative pockets on the skirt front. I picked out the stitches the night before and removed them, but the shadow of the pockets remained; much worse than the actual pockets. I looked shabby. Shabby and fat.

I didn't really. I looked okay, like who I was: a young teenager going to school in a skirt and blouse.

I didn't recognize it enough at the time, but this school cost money. While my parents identified as "comfortable," it must have been a strain.

Years later, my mother told me about going to her bank and getting bonds out of her safety-deposit box to use as collateral for a loan to send me to Camp Stanley. She described the edges as "frayed" because of the number of times she'd removed/replaced them to borrow money. Another thing I wish I'd known at the time. I might have been less of an ingrate.

* * *

My first day at Weston, Dad dropped me off. I was nervous, but he'd been soothing and supportive on the drive in. Mrs. Lewis met me, we had a few words in her office and she led me up the stairs to the second floor with most of the classrooms. All the girls were already in class.

Mrs. Lewis kept up her kindly stream of chat about when recess was, and how school secretary Mrs. Clarke would ring the bell, and then she stood in front of a classroom door with her hand on the handle.

She said, "It turns out I don't have enough room in grade eight, Moira, so I'm putting you in grade nine." Then she opened the door and ushered me in. Once again, I was appropriately speechless at suddenly finding myself having skipped a grade. I'm thirteen and in ninth grade and in the middle of what would come to be known as the October Crisis.

I keep it to myself that I came from eighth grade in a suburban Catholic public school. I later realized no one would really have cared. The girls in my small ninth-grade class were mostly from fairly wealthy homes, and many were troubled homes, to varying degrees. I felt their eyes on me as a girl at the back made room for me at her table. I later learned she had room at her table because the other girls didn't like her, and isolated her.

One girl I loathed the minute I clapped eyes on her. Later, she became one of my best friends and remains so to this day. I hated her then because she was blonde and pretty. She told me later she hated me because "I could tell you were smart." It turned out our fathers had known each other in school and then in the army. But that meant nothing when we were in ninth grade and hating it—and each other.

This friend had difficulty in school, mostly due to undiagnosed dyslexia. While silently hating her, I admired the way she played the system, such as wearing a blouse that wasn't the regulation blue and being sent home to get changed. Both her parents worked, so she lollygagged on her way home, changed her blouse, then stopped at Murray's restaurant on Sherbrooke Street for lunch on her return trip. We bungled through that year, not being friends. She went to another school in tenth grade and landed back at Weston the next year, due to poor grades and undisciplined shenanigans.

This grade-skip was a prime example of genius carrot-and-stick psychology. Mrs. Lewis handed me what I had so rudely requested (the next step to get the fuck out of high school) and had put me in a situation where I had to actually do the schoolwork to get what I wanted (to grow up, graduate, and leave home ASAP) because Weston's secondary programs were so different from the school where I had been.

Ninth-grade math at Weston was algebra, which I'd never studied. French was more advanced than the curriculum I was used to. For physical education, we had to go to a gym at another facility, and I managed to evade that. But even for the stuff I found easy, like English and history, I was behind, so I had to concentrate and get to work—and find my slot in this odd little group of square pegs at this strange little school.

I hated, hated, *hated* going to Weston at the time, but I have so often since been grateful. It supported me with baseline consistency in difficult times, without the people involved necessarily knowing how weird my life was. It showed me women who ran things. For me, the school normalized women and girls being smart. And getting good marks.

And scholarships. And being on the debate team. And the McGill public speaking team. And finding a way to internal and external acceptance, even with some spectacular fails along the way.

As I was trying to find my place among the square pegs, the FLQ terrorists had either been arrested or sent to Cuba, and Canada had scaled back from full-on martial law when my mother sprang Camp Stanley on me in 1971.

* * *

When talking about my childhood chubbiness or obesity, people will ask me if I was always fat or always felt fat. I think of one particular photo when I say, "No. I wasn't fat when I was little."

The photo I think of is one of my favorites: a Christmas photo of me and my sister in front of our fireplace, after the gift-opening carnage has been resolved. She is sitting on a footstool, her legs crossed at the ankles; I am standing to her right. We are both dressed in party dresses of blue velvet and holding our Christmas gift "bride dolls," hers blonde, mine brunette, each about one foot tall. She is holding hers with one hand at the doll's back, I am holding mine right in front of me, by the arms, wearing a teeth-gritted grin as though I feared Christmas aliens might swoop down and whisk her away from me. My sister and I both had curled hair, thanks to a night spent sleeping in soft curlers known as "Spoolies."

I look at this photo and think: *what a happy little girl with her big sister.* I see an easy smile, and none of the "baby fat" Mason sees as a prelude to childhood and adult obesity. I see a solid physique with sturdy legs, ready to smile and laugh and run and play and swim and climb and dance.

I love to dance; always have and still do: ballet, jazz, contemporary, tap, flamenco. I was lucky to take ballet lessons Saturday morning at the neighborhood school and to perform at annual recitals. I learned so much more than ballet in those classes, learning the positions with piano accompaniment and repetitive steps. I learned how to follow directions, how to listen to music, how to listen to the directions given by the music, how to dance in relation to other dancers, how to breathe, and to always keep a face cloth and a spare pair of tights in your dance bag.

One early costume was a long tutu in sea-foam green with purple sequins on the shoulder straps and purple flowers at the waist with purple petals sprinkled on the skirt. This was the one mentioned earlier, created for me by Mrs. Kindly Eastern European Seamstress. We wore artificial purple flowers in our hair, lashed to hair combs with thread.

My mother was a whiz when it came to costume creation with crepe paper. She transformed me into a sunflower one year, with a costume of yellow and green, and into a "Spanish dancer" another year, a look I specifically requested. In my mind, I had conflated Gypsy clichés with flamenco stereotypes, so my mother made me a cotton skirt with a "tail" (a *bata de cola* wannabe), layered with multi-colored crepe paper ruffles she *stapled* to the cotton. I made a "tambourine" out of an aluminum takeout container filled with buttons, with ribbons trailing.

As good as she was as a costumer, she contracted out the green-and-purple confection. She came home with the green shiny satin for the bodice, the tulle for the skirt, the flowers made of soft cardboard and the sequins, then announced we'd be going to visit Mrs. Kindly Eastern European Seamstress, who lived about two blocks away.

On our first visit, Mrs. Kindly Seamstress looked at the fabric and the sketch and nodded. She took a bunch of measurements of me and then told my mother the date for my next "fitting."

When we returned, I was delighted by how she had transformed the shiny satin and scratchy tulle and the sparkly sequins into an actual outfit, a tutu, a *costume*. It had a zipper up the back, which, undone, allowed for this confection to be lowered over my upstretched arms and pulled down over my boxy childlike torso and zipped up the back to contain me.

There was no mirror to check my appearance, but I felt different. Way, way different. I had been a bit disappointed that this performance hadn't required what I considered a true tutu, one that fanned out from the hips like an upside-down saucer. This skirt was more like a bell and came to about my knees. With my arms bare, I felt an ease of movement. My mother agreed the costume fit well; all that needed finessing was the length of the shoulder straps before the sequins were affixed. The straps had been tentatively pinned in place for the fitting.

The two women negotiated the correct length of the shoulder straps and checked with me for comfort confirmation. This led to the fleeting pin-stab and the description of me as "well-upholstered." I have long maintained this didn't bother me but note how clear the memory is.

A few days after my brilliant performance at the big recital, I did a matinee at the school and took the bus home. There had been no face cloth or cold cream to wipe off the swipe of rouge and dash of lipstick. I felt grown up and full of performance endorphins. I took the longer bus route so I could enjoy this feeling. I actually heard someone say, "Look at the little kid wearing makeup." I thought I was grown up and fair grand; I had no idea I was worrying my mother and grandmother by not being home in good time.

* * *

In primary school, I slowly realized I was a bit chonkier than my peers, thanks to some intermittent physical "fails" that undermined my self-confidence, and some revelations elsewhere.

I had trouble in gym class, a weekly hour of torture I avoided by feigning illness and/or injury. My school didn't have a proper gym, so we had gym class in the assembly hall with hard, hard floors that had the stage at one end and the laughable cafeteria at the other. I was very good on the balance beam and anything related to what I learned in my Saturday dance class. The cheerleaders looked as though they had some dance moves, but I was still too little for that. I later made the mistake of wondering aloud about being a cheerleader, and never heard the end of it from one fat girl with a beautiful mane of blonde hair and a mean disposition.

In the third grade, I was elected by my classmates to star in our year-end production of *Snow White*. The homemade costume appeared after I picked out the stitches in the hem of a discarded dirndl skirt my sister had made for herself so it was a long skirt on me. In the first act, I knelt on stage in front of a mirror masquerading as a pond, and sang "I'm Wishing."

While I loved the star turn, I would have preferred to sing "Whistle While you Work" and "Heigh-Ho. It's Off to Work We Go" with the chorus of dwarves. Way more fun.

A male schoolmate, who was fat himself, once called me "fatty fatty, two by four." Another compared me to a London double-decker bus when I wore a new, red, drop-waisted Terylene dress with a white collar. I loved that dress and wore it with white tights—but I had no bosom yet, so I did look like a red block.

I got a beautiful bike, a green three-speed, for my tenth birthday. I loved feeling my skin cool down as I got up to speed and created a breeze. My weakness was heading over to the drugstore at 45th Avenue in Lachine (the Montreal suburb where I grew up) for comic books and later magazines (*Tiger Beat*), salt-and-vinegar potato chips and chocolate bars. I also liked going to the Lysanne bakery for palmiers (elephant ears) and mille-feuilles pastries. One schoolmate who lived nearby would taunt me about my junk-food purchases, so I learned to hide them.

Once, on vacation in Maine, we were staying at a family-friendly cottage compound and I looked around for some pals my own age. There was one girl there who stared me down when I greeted her. She then circled me twice before asking: "How much do you weigh?" A strange response, I thought, to "Hi! What's your name?"

It also stung. I felt cornered by an absolute stranger, and I didn't know how to react. I would later learn absolute strangers often chose to comment on things that were none of their business.

CHAPTER 2

Before: those damn jeans (and genes)

"Is your child using food as a weapon? ... You know your child better than anyone else does. If you watch his actions and think about his situation, you should be able to get a pretty good idea of whether or not your child is punishing you by getting fat."
—Gussie Mason

I didn't feel fat as a little girl. I was well-fed by my grandmother and active with my friends. I got freshly squeezed orange juice for breakfast and oatmeal or eggs and toast.

Life was playing outside with neighborhood friends. Tag, hopscotch, skipping, statues (a game where you spun around and froze in position), swing sets, and teeter-totters. That feeling as though I could run like the wind because I was light as a feather in the spring, when I was finally able to remove my boots. For several winters, I (sort of) skated on the backyard rink my father built.

Our family doctor gave me a talk one day about how if I had the choice between two crackers or one, I should choose just one. I didn't understand why he was pointing this out to me.

His waiting room had the classical music station from Plattsburgh on. There was a B&W photo of a lovely woman; my eight-year-old deductive reasoning figured it must be his wife. I also inferred that she was dead. Again, why were we at his office? And why were we discussing my weight?

The doctor asked if I ever didn't want to go out, if I was depressed and didn't want people to see me because of my weight. I don't remember my response. I was depressed, but not because of my weight. I was depressed because my grandmother had died and I seemed to be the only one who noticed.

Any weight increase was easier to hide by wearing a school uniform, a dark blue V-neck tunic with a fabric self-belt with two button positions. There was no waist band to roll, no button atop a zipper at the waist. I would just strain the tunic's seams with any increasing girth, or preclude the buttoning of the lower buttons on the white blouse I wore underneath.

* * *

My dad was able to gain or lose twenty pounds in what seemed like a heartbeat. A diet was always imminent when his little calorie-counter booklet appeared, pink and black with its spine reinforced in black electrical tape. He had yogurt delivered, made locally and arriving in stubby, thick glass jars with cardboard lids, like you had on an ice-cream cone retrieved from a corner-store freezer. This was his go-to dessert when dieting; he would peel off the lid and spill a bit of maple syrup on top, slicing the surface with his spoon and watching the golden fluid disappear in the milky crevasse.

Dad made a great breakfast for himself before work and for me sometimes on weekends. He liked a poached or soft-boiled egg and toast, eaten while he read the *Montreal Gazette* and drank a mug of tea. He often went out for lunch at restaurants in downtown Montreal; he enjoyed good food and was a gourmand without being a snob.

My father taught me how to eat in a restaurant. He told me if I was indecisive to order something I'd never had before. What if I don't like it? Then send it back. Say to the waiter: "This isn't what I expected. May I please see the menu again so I can order something else? I'll happily pay for this but I can't eat it." I've only done this a few times, but I've never paid for a meal I couldn't eat. Dad taught me how to enjoy pomegranate. Kumquats. Arctic char. These were rare, exotic treats in late-sixties suburban Montreal.

My Mum was petite and slender. She sometimes complained of a "jumpy tummy"; she would sit on the couch and rock, sometimes with a hot water bottle clamped to the abdomen. She spent a lot of time in the bathroom. I think she was probably suffering from undiagnosed IBS or IBD. Her appetite would sometimes disappear, and she'd only be able to nibble on saltines or dry white toast.

In tandem with Dad's dieting was exercise. He was a runner and a weight lifter, having been an amateur boxer in the army. Later, when I discovered strength training, he and I would go to the Y together, where he taught me weight-room etiquette that served me well: if you're just resting between sets, claim a bench with a towel. Offer to spot another lifter. Always wipe down the equipment. Return plates to the rack. Courtesy will take you far.

The gym was home to a number of Montreal's Black fighters. At first, they thought we were the oddest of odd couples, the old white guy and the young chick. They chuckled behind our backs. After a while, they figured out we were father and daughter, and that normalized our status somewhat. When I started to go every day, executing a split routine and working with a trainer, things changed again. They saw I was serious.

At first, some did mean things, like leaving the giant, heavy plates on the weight-lifting machines so I would have to ask for help to get them off. Snicker, snicker.

So I asked for help. And I got it. I continued to execute my reps and sets, getting stronger and leaner.

When it became clear I was serious, the fighters became my biggest allies. They loved that I came with my dad and that I came alone. Weight training and a Y membership was a great gift from my father, along with a similar metabolism.

I discussed competition with the trainer there. The film *Pumping Iron II: The Women* had just come out and I thought it worth investigating. I tried to follow the pre-competition regime he suggested, but I didn't last. I was dizzy and headache-y by the first afternoon, and realized I didn't want to compete. The posing was a bit much, and I didn't want to feel hungry and awful. I knew how much I could lift.

After my first training regime in the mid-1980s, I stayed slim and active in the sport for some time. One of my best physiques had me at 160 pounds, a size nine, and cut. I stayed that way even when travel and job changes altered my routine. The fashion then was carb-loading, so I did that intermittently—yet didn't suffer speedy weight gain when I wasn't training.

* * *

There are no photos of my pregnant mother. There was one, at a kiddie birthday party, where a lady near term was handing out cake, but we only saw her from the shoulders down, so there was no guarantee it was my mother.

My lovely slender mother, who didn't eat when upset. She also smoked, telling me once she had decided long before she was old enough that she would smoke. She smoked right up until the end, and, when she still lived alone, didn't tell her family of emphysema and COPD diagnoses. She said a cigarette was one little perk she could look forward to—until she couldn't.

When she was older, she became dangerously thin a few times—"Boost" territory, as my brother called it. She drank her food supplement chilled, in a red wine glass. My brother also observed that there was one thing you could always get Mum to eat: a ham sandwich on white bread with mayo and the crusts cut off, the sandwich cut into triangles. Maybe with a few potato chips or celery sticks.

* * *

Exercise? Mum? No. Although I knew she had been active in her youth, having heard stories about weekends spent skiing up north.

* * *

When I was in the sixth grade, I went to a Christmas party at a classmate's house. We were down in the basement TV room, listening to records and eating chips and dip, little sandwiches, sausage rolls, all that salty, fatty, party stuff. I wore the A-line green-velvet dress with a stand-up collar and puffed sleeves I had made. My mother's circular silver pin with pearls at the front of the stand-up collar, at my throat. I was wearing white tights.

The food was presented buffet-style on a series of foldable TV tables with tray tops painted with floral scenes. There were Christmas tunes and current pop music on the record player, and some games that would engage eleven-year-old girls. Nothing interested me until the dancing started. I did like to dance, but even that didn't last too long. I just wanted to get home. Looking back, that was the dichotomy: I couldn't wait to grow up and leave, and I couldn't wait to get home when I was out.

We were in our socks and I hated being without shoes—still do. I set myself in a chair with a TV table laden with chips and dip while we played Secret Santa. I overloaded a Maple Leaf potato chip with dip and, on the voyage to my mouth, dropped a big glop on my green-velvet dress.

Did I take the time to scrape up the dip delicately, and leave it with my napkin? Or did I scrape it up and pop it in my non-discriminating mouth? All I remember is hearing someone say: "All you want to do is eat."

Correct as the observation was, I didn't say anything and I felt embarrassed.

She was not far off, I fear. Chips and chocolate were largely verboten in our house, as all three kids suffered acne when it was believed to have a dietary cause. Chips were not often in the house for the same reason—they were junk food—and because some of us (such as myself) would thoughtlessly "fill up on chips" if left to our own devices after school.

* * *

There was a lot of family turmoil in the winter of 1969. In February, my dear older brother experienced an "event": a psychotic break? A breakdown? It was later referred to as "when Ronnie had to go to the hospital." He was taken away in an ambulance after a night of shouting that had started with tears. I was told to stay in my parents' downstairs bedroom. I could hear voices yelling and crying and crashes, but not words. Some of it was tinged with fear, some with rage, some with despair. I kneeled in front of the crucifix in my parents' bedroom, alone, trying to drown out the yelling with meaningless incantation of Hail Marys and Our Fathers. The sound died down a bit only to ramp up again with sounds of doors being opened and two new voices entering the choir.

My father was directing the paramedics through the front door and upstairs to my brother's bedroom.

The voices became less angry and scared. I could hear my brother "joshing" with one of the paramedics, the way he did so well to put people at ease. His words made little sense and were spoken at an inappropriately high volume, an indication of his ongoing distress. The paramedic's voice was lower and soothing. I heard the front door close, and then the ambulance door. Then it was quiet and I waited for a cue about what to do next.

"Crimson and Clover" by Tommy James and the Shondells was on the radio. I liked it then, but I hate it now because it always takes me back to that night.

There was a knock on the bedroom door and my mother came in. She said my brother had been taken to the hospital and that my father had followed in our car. She then said she was going to make some tea.

She gave me a soothing, vague explanation of what had happened. I could see inside my brother's room: furniture shoved around, books on the floor, clothing and bed linens strewn about. My mother quickly pulled his door shut, but not before I registered the chaos. My pinpoint memory is a yellow, plastic BBQ sauce container in the room. Later, after Ron's room had been cleaned, I asked her what that had been doing there. I give her credit for not lying to me or obfuscating. She said they had called Ron's psychiatrist during the incident, and he instructed them to get Ron to take some of his pills. Ron refused and gritted his teeth; they were afraid he might bite a water glass and be hurt, so the plastic BBQ sauce container was used instead. I don't remember if they were successful.

I didn't go to school the next day, or for the rest of the week. I overheard my mother calling the school, gently explaining why I hadn't finished an assignment. It was an assignment I was upset about not finishing, because I loved the story and thought I was so clever in how I was telling it: a patchwork quilt with each piece of fabric a door into a person's story or an event.

I don't remember how she circumlocuted Ron's "event," because an ambulance at our house in the middle of the night would have made the gossip rounds like wildfire. The ensuing winter weeks were stark and strange, with my brother not at home.

* * *

I envied one particular classmate in sixth grade. She wasn't smarter or richer or prettier or any of the things I might have envied. No, I just got it into my head that this classmate didn't have to deal with being teased for being fat by other fat children. She didn't have to deal with an ambulance coming to get her brother. She probably didn't ache with loneliness for her grandmother. One day, when I was feeling soggy and couldn't maintain my exterior boundary, I blurted all this out at my mother when she had been foolish enough to ask me: "How are you doing, my wee chicken?"

Mine wasn't a weeping blurt, more of a tight-throated quavering bleat. She just listened, sat thoughtfully for a moment and said: "Nobody's life is perfect, and I don't think you can make those assumptions about your classmate. None of us can ever really know the burdens of another, but we must remember others *have* burdens. We can never guess the troubles of another."

Then she gave me an Olympic-caliber hug.

CHAPTER 3
Blindsided

The young girl, twelve or thirteen years old, is seated cross-legged and staring off, over the photographer's left shoulder. She's wearing one of those sixties-style kerchiefs, a fabric triangle with strings we wore to keep our hair out of our eyes. It was blue with white trim, and she has a lovely drape of dark brown hair. She is smiling. She has a tennis racket across her lap and she's peeling an orange; small scraps of *peau d'orange* are arranged on the racket's webbing, as though they were nesting bowls. I can almost smell the refreshing citrus fragrance across time and space. I even wonder about how the citric acid in the orange peel and fruit segments might dissolve the racket webbing.

Also in this brochure are regular pairs of before-and-after B&W photos of campers. In the before photos, the girls, unsmiling, are usually in one-piece bathing suits, with hands on hips, staring at the camera. They tend to be smiling in the after photo, wearing a garment much more flattering, designed to show off the weight loss. Sometimes a three-quarter turn and model-like posture is employed to the same effect. These photos accompany testimonials from the camper or her family.

The brochure also provides a daily schedule of swimming, tennis, "Slimnastics," golf, rest, meals, and snacks.

I pored over some of the other photos: girls with beanbags on their heads, descending a three-step box with a woman holding their hands lightly for balance. Girls setting up to putt on the golf course, girls eating at banquet tables, wearing lots of color for reasons I couldn't discern, girls in a musical theater production, girls swimming, girls doing archery, girls playing soccer, girls playing baseball—and a girl with her back to me on a doctor's scale being manipulated by a smiling adult.

The weekly and monthly routines involved events such as talent shows, fashion shows, putting on an abridged musical, and in late August something called Color War, where the whole camp was attached to a color and teams competed for prizes and pride.

It all looked exhausting on several levels. To me, a thirteen-year-old introvert, all that time spent with others and not spent alone in my room reading was just too much.

The cover was a wide shot of a green golf course, with a girl golfer and another holding a flag on the green. The Camp Stanley logo was there in white. Everybody looked happy. They were all well-lit, which made the environment look sunny and warm there in the Catskills. Hurleyville, New York, to be precise.

My mother pulled this brochure out of its white postal envelope and started a parental monologue about how I would enjoy it, how it would be a chance to get away from home, spend a whole summer in the country, at camp: "Since, as you know, Daddy and I won't be here for much of the summer and we want you to have a good time."

Ah. So that's what's going on. I knew already they were going to Europe for Dad's business plus a summer holiday and I was only slightly disappointed I hadn't been invited; I was at the age when holidaying with your parents was getting boring, even though I often got to go fishing in Lake Champlain or experience summer-stock Shakespeare or surfing in the ocean off Ogunquit, Maine, or food I'd never had before. I was the youngest of three and we'd had our last family vacation to Europe in 1966, after my grandmother had died and just before my brother went to college.

I had been looking forward to having the house to myself, although I couldn't be left completely alone in 1971, given my age. Perhaps my sister would come home (she was living in her own place near the McGill campus downtown) or Mum would engage a family friend to stay with me. With these two possibilities I could quite easily avoid too much interference and still be minimally polite. Although when I think of it now, I cringe and then burn with shame for being such a self-absorbed, entitled little jerk.

What would I have done all by myself all summer? Stay up late. Watch TV, tuned into the US stations out of Plattsburgh, New York, and Burlington, Vermont (they came in better late at night). Play my records too loud and dance. Sleep in. Eat whatever, whenever (lots of toast and cheese). Go to the pool, where, despite being good swimmer, I was so nervous about taking a test I still had a diamond-shaped "non-swimmer badge" sewn on to my navy-blue one-piece with a modesty panel. I was a good swimmer, but I didn't like to be tested.

If it was hot I would sleep in the cool basement. I would lie on my father's workout bench and study my reflection in the mirror he had placed overhead, held aloft by the pattern of water pipes. He used it to check his form when bench-pressing. I liked how gravity made my face look more articulated, thinner.

I tuned out my mother's monologue, but not before I heard her say she'd arranged a call with the camp director, Gussie Mason, so I could ask her any questions I might have. Immediately incensed, I said something rude, something like: "Well, I don't have any questions because I'm not going." Then I walked out the door.

I heard her calling me, the anger in her voice increasing along with the volume. It started to fade as I got farther and farther away, down the street. I ran out barefoot. I was wearing a short-sleeved summer print dress in yellow tones that buttoned up the front, with a stand-up collar. It was suppertime, early evening, mid- to late spring, so it got cool quickly after the sun went down. I headed toward the lake. Now anger had overtaken me; I felt "nauseous," my heart was pounding and I was crying.

I headed toward our church, Resurrection of Our Lord. I tried the door to the church hall, the door I used to get in Saturday afternoons for folk-group practice, or as we prepared for a Sunday morning coffee shop, run by young parishioners. It was locked. I sat on the stone steps, where, seated, I could get close enough to the hem of my dress to wipe my eyes. I then pulled my dress over my knees and I tried to get warm. I sat there and rocked, trying not to cry anymore, with middling success.

I considered ringing the bell at the rectory, to see if I could get help from one of our parish priests, but I knew their first move would be a call to my mother. Then I remembered my friend who lived between the church and my house. Surely she would listen and make me a cup of tea.

This friend was a few years ahead of me in school, in the youth group that oversaw the Sunday morning coffee shop at church, and was a favorite student of my mother's. She had younger brothers and a wonderful mother from the Maritimes. I persuaded myself, in a stellar example of not thinking things through, that she might let me hide out at her place, even sleep on the couch.

I knocked on the screen door and her mum directed me to where my friend was watching TV. The minute I saw her, I burst into tears. She was used to my drama-queeniness; many a Sunday morning while prepping big urns of coffee for church, I'd had teary outbursts over guys. She gave me a hug and some Kleenex and made me a cup of tea.

She let me talk through my hiccupping sobs, outlining the story, and then directed me to finish my tea, wipe my face with the cool washcloth she handed me, go home and apologize to my mother.

Apologize! My ... my mother was the one sending ME away, SHE should be apologizing. This is what I thought, but I silently nodded as I handed the facecloth back. I knew an apology was my only way out—and my only way back into the warm house where I lived.

My friend hugged me and pushed me out the door, making me promise to let her know how things went, assuring me it would be okay.

I started to shiver walking home barefoot in the gathering dark. I didn't really know how to frame my apology. I walked into the house and sat again on the same spot at the end of the couch. I turned on the TV, to its comforting white noise.

My mother entered the room. I looked up and was about to say something when she hit me on the shoulder with a rolled-up newspaper. She started a hoarse stream of invective about walking out when she was talking to me and letting her worry, not knowing where I was, and how dare I speak to her that way. My response, after shocked silence, was to stand and yell: "Stop hitting me, stop hitting me, stop hitting me!"

I tried to get away, moving sideways and then backing up, but she followed and kept yelling. She grabbed at my clothing and hit me with a weak-wristed open hand. With her other hand, she kept hitting me with the rolled-up newspaper, closer now to my face. I felt like a dog, being whacked for peeing on the carpet. When I could back up no farther, her open hand made contact with the skin on my arm. I grabbed my mother by the wrists. We stopped moving.

"Let me go," she yelled.

"No! If I let you go, you'll keep hitting me."

I could have hurt her. She was a petite woman and even at my age, I was taller than she was, and certainly heavier.

She had certainly hurt *me*, wanting to send me away to a slim-down camp for girls.

I don't remember exactly how we negotiated a bloodless end, where I let go without fear of being hit anymore by a rolled-up newspaper and a stream of verbal rage.

The next thing I actually remember is being upstairs in my room, after crying and trying not to barf and hearing my dad's car come home, him entering the house, my parent's voices in their downstairs bedroom. Their vocal modulation wasn't that of a fight, or a reporting-and-listening. There was no laughter, a hallmark of most of their discussions. I heard my father's voice a little more than I heard my mother's, near the end. Then my dad came up the stairs and gently knocked on my door.

He was gentle, accommodating, and comforting in a don't-worry-it-will-all-work-out kind of way. He did insist in a low-key, non-threatening way, that I apologize to my mother.

"You and your mother can't deal with each other like that."

I started to sputter about *unfairness and how she started it and I only grabbed her because she was hitting me and…* He stopped me.

"I've said the same to your mother, that was no way to deal with each other. And you will apologize to her.

"But not tonight," he added, before asking if I was hungry.

I nodded yes, and he brought me a cup of tea and piece of cinnamon toast, a rare treat when not at the cottage. It was his acknowledgment of the gravity of the evening's events and the need to return to some kind of domestic homeostasis.

* * *

I had a near-sleepless night filled with rage, fear, adrenalin. It gave me lots of time to think. I woke up with my hips and my head aching. I was also developing a paranoid streak after the October Crisis the previous autumn, as well as an accidental air-raid siren very early one morning in that summer. This nameless dread flattened me on the floor of my room anytime I heard a siren or even a car driving fast by my house late at night. I was convinced I would be sprayed by gunfire coming from the speeding car. Too much time spent watching *The F.B.I*.

What happened next? I must have apologized and wept, and I'm sure my mother did the same thing. Isn't this what happens when women fight? Mothers and daughters? Any kind of long-lasting estrangement is unthinkable in most circumstances.

I parsed what I might have said that started the fight so I could make any apology very specific. I probably overthought it, decided it was my refusal to take the phone call that had been the problem and apologized for that.

There was ultimately a long-distance phone call with Camp Stanley owner Gussie Mason. I was on my mother's white princess phone, sitting on Dad's side of the bed in their master bedroom.

I perceived her having an insincere tone; it was something I experienced often coming from adults. From Mason, it was a mix of sales pitch and condescension.

I had matured physically, menstruating and growing breasts ahead of many of my social contemporaries and classmates. That's why, at the end of her sales pitch to a reticent camper, I asked to be in a bunk with older girls.

"No, absolutely not."

I was shocked by the definitive denial. Silenced, in fact. I think Mason took that as agreement. She said, "Tell your mother I'll be in touch." I meant my silence to mean: *The deal is off, I'm not spending a summer camping with little girls.*

My mother had given me "the menstruation talk" and "the sex talk." I remember bursting into tears after the latter. I give my mother credit; she might have been a bit uptight—she didn't want me to have sex outside of marriage and get hurt—but she gave me the straight goods, all the information I needed to avoid pregnancy and STDs. She acknowledged my precocity, physical and otherwise, by swearing me to secrecy, very specifically: "I don't want you talking to This Friend or That Friend, because their mothers may not have talked to them about it yet, and they don't need to hear it from you." She told me to come to her with any questions, even telling me not to ask my sister.

Following my unsatisfactory conversation with Gussie Mason, I realized how tiring it is to fight.

CHAPTER 4

Surrender: then what?

> "For children in early adolescence, nothing counts more than appearances. And I don't think there is anything in the world more cruel than the way young adolescents treat each other."
> —*Gussie Mason*

I completely capitulated.

I had fought and fought and created lists of conditions and then finally one day, in my room, as I listened to my father make yet another reasoned argument—leavened with a bit of bribery, how he'd paint my room while I was gone—I was suddenly just so tired. I had no agency, really, in this situation. When that finally landed on my quotidian consciousness, my unconditional surrender and a limp/hopeless feeling followed.

"Okay, Dad, I'll go." My father hugged me, took my head in both his hands and gave me a full-frontal Dad-peck on the lips. "It's the right thing, you'll see," he said. The smell of Neet hair-removal cream was in the air; I'm returned to that moment anytime I get a whiff of that depilatory chemical smell.

I was a precocious adolescent with older siblings, and I'd lobbied hard to be in a bunk with older girls. Gussie Mason refused, but said

I'd be with the eldest girls in my age group. I had to settle; she'd hung up the phone pretty fast.

I told my friends I was going to camp, no further details. Only the friend whose home I'd run to barefoot the night my mother and I nearly had the fistfight was told everything. I was worried I'd be surrounded by "little girls," but in fact I made friends in my own age group, all of us dealing with varying levels of largely unarticulated self-loathing, loneliness, fear, hunger, fatigue, alienation, and rage.

* * *

Two of the many things required for Camp Stanley were golf clubs: a low number and a high number, not quite a driver and a putter/chipper. I went shopping at a sporting-goods store with my mother and was shocked when she assumed an expert stance with the putter and offered the salesperson an assessment of how it felt.

Turns out my mother played both golf and tennis quite a bit in her youth—and with some skill, according to my father. She had also been a skier. Because I knew nothing about golf, I would accept her direction, showing me how to hold a club and execute a swing.

You think you know your mother, but you didn't know her before she made you. And you didn't know she knew how to play golf! I only ever pictured her with a schoolbag, or at the dining-room table surrounded by "corrections" and "prep." She was either working assiduously at the demands of being a high-school English teacher, or typing up papers: her own for one of her many night-school classes, or my brother's college papers, or my father's speeches.

Her reading would keep her up late at night, sitting in the wing chair from my paternal grandmother's house, her feet up on the matching hassock, a notebook on the chair arm, her ashtray overflowing.

It was later she would sometimes make herself an Amer Picon in a crystal glass to drink as she read: crème de cassis, soda water, and the liquor slid into a glass over a spoon, making stripes of varying densities.

At some point Mum started to regularly have more than one drink. She would yell at me up the stairs. Sometimes I heard Dad come out to quieten her, soothe her, and persuade her to go to bed. I still had trouble getting back to sleep. I didn't get many full nights' sleep in high school.

* * *

My Mum bought me a tennis racket for camp, a red-and-white one with a spring frame press. This worked well for me, playing tennis against the board at Carignan Park. Even when she colluded with me to skip school due to my frequent headaches, she was okay with me taking my racket up the street to play off the board. I never asked for lessons or sought out other players; I didn't realize doubles tennis was a thing. My tennis style was goofy and undisciplined, not designed to win or even improve—much like backyard badminton with my Dad.

I started staying up all night Saturdays sewing or reading and then leaving the house early to go to church. Then one day I went to the park with my racket and started to whack balls off the board.

I was alone. Out of the corner of my eye, I spotted a fellow approach. He was disheveled-looking, with bedhead and shoved-on sweats. He was very kind, but explained how tennis wasn't, in fact, permitted this early in the morning, particularly on weekends, when people might be trying to sleep in. The sound could be heard in every house ringing the park, he pointed out. This had never occurred to me, so I apologized and put my racket back in its press.

I went to sit on the swings, as I didn't want to go home. Before I knew it, a police car pulled up near the park not far from me. Again, a very kind policeman asked what I was doing there at that hour. I explained I had been playing tennis against myself but a neighbor told me I was too early. The police officer agreed, and told me to go home. He stayed in his car until I left the park.

I realize now my late nights and early mornings out were to ensure no surprises could wake me up from a sound sleep, where I might be unprepared. Drama. Tears. Yelling. Air-raid sirens. The army surrounding the house, looking for a kidnapped cabinet minister. Real or imagined gunfire from a passing car. Whatever it was, I wanted to be awake and ready.

* * *

My teenage fear and paranoia went from accelerated heartbeats to a bit of breathlessness, sweating, even: it was top-tier fight-or-flight. Why? I grew up in a Montreal suburb, roof over my head, clothes on my back, food in my tummy. I went to Catholic school, lucky enough to learn French at an early age. (I thought it was all the same language until I was eight or nine.) I did get teased sometimes for being fat, other times for being smart. ("What did you do, swallow a dictionary?") Or because my mother was a teacher ("Mummy's a teacher so you get good grades!").

Just into my teens, simply by having hips and breasts, I was also dealing with newly attracted attention: some of it I appreciated because it made me feel grown up. But most of it was unwanted.

* * *

Quebec didn't celebrate Victoria Day on the May 24 weekend (when Americans have Memorial Day). Because of the province's French roots, it waits a month, until June 21, for Fête de la St Jean: St. Jean Baptiste Day. During the late sixties and early seventies, the holiday was marked by nationalist riots.

At the 1968 St. Jean Baptiste Day parade, Prime Minister Pierre Elliott Trudeau had stood firm when threatened while in the grandstand. He leaned on one elbow at the front of his box, waving off his security. That image stuck with me.

I wasn't ghoulish, but my inner Lois Lane paid attention to the news, probably because my father did and he spoke of it at the dinner table.

My sister was caught downtown during one of the St. Jean Baptiste day riots. We were all concerned until she sailed in the door just before supper. She'd seen what was shaping up and wisely found her way home. I heard other tales of people trying to get home just as the looting started, and how tempting it was if you found yourself outside a store just as windows were being smashed and the early summer light was failing.

After a few years of riots downtown, Fête celebrations were moved to Mount Royal. I once watched a couple necking on the grass there: vigorously, ferociously. Had they not been surrounded by revelers, they would likely have progressed to the next level. My mother spotted me staring and hustled me along.

In 1976, while I was working at the *Gazette*, I dated a cab driver named Ted Leja. The first time we met, he drove me in silence to my suburban home and started a conversation when he saw my father's car adorned with scuba decals. By the end of the chat, I'd paid my cab fare and we had a date.

We went for dinner at the Mazurka, a Polish restaurant on Prince Arthur in the Plateau. It was hearty, inexpensive, tasty fare. We talked and laughed. I knew it wasn't going to be serious, but we had fun.

I have a photo of Ted and me and my best friend, taken by her boyfriend. We're on Crescent Street and we girls were holding roses that have been purchased for us by our dates. We were laughing, laughing, laughing and it's clear we'd been drinking. We hadn't yet proceeded to being belligerent or obnoxious drunks. It was the Olympic summer of 1976 and the vibe in Montreal was feeling kind of crowded, very European and world-class because people were there from all over the globe.

Ted and I had lots of no-commitment fun: Montreal nightlife, dinners out, watching bad movies on the TV at the apartment he shared with a couple of roommates. I was heading back to school in Ottawa come September. Even so, I learned that Ted's father lived in the Ste-Anne-de-Bellevue Veterans Hospital because of the non-lethal but life-altering injuries he had suffered while trying to defuse an FLQ mailbox bomb on May 17, 1963. The FLQ viewed the postal service as a symbol of modern-day English colonial power.

Sgt.-Maj. Walter Leja had been doing his job as a bomb-disposal expert at a mailbox on Sherbrooke Street at Lansdowne Avenue in Westmount. It was one of a series of fifteen mailbox bombs placed by the terrorists. Several went off at 3 a.m., others were dismantled.

Leja, then forty-two, lost his hand and suffered other injuries to his chest and face. His survival was in doubt but he pulled through, living until 1992. The photograph taken almost immediately after the blast is famous. It's pretty graphic and wasn't published as part of the coverage of the event. It was published two months later, after it won an award for the *Gazette* photographer who took it, Garth Pritchard.

"There was a great bang and pieces of the mailbox went flying over my head," Pritchard said, in a story published the day after the award. "There were clouds of black and white smoke. When the smoke started to clear, I saw him lying in the street. It was so quiet you could have heard a pin drop."

Years later, my new boyfriend (now husband), an American, asked me, when we were dating in Montreal: why is it you always want to cross the street when we get near a mailbox?

CHAPTER 5

Division Four bunk life: food, follies, friends, and exercise

"It's still difficult for some parents to accept that the chubby little boy who keeps stuffing himself may actually be undernourished. Those goodies he devours have little or no food value."
—Gussie Mason

I never thought my entire life could be stuffed in a duffel bag. But when you're shipped off—or rather taken there in an early-seventies model Oldsmobile—to camp in the Catskills, that's a given.

At Camp Stanley, I was in Division Four, Bunk "L." We got to pick a name for the bunk: we chose "Light 'n' Lively," which was also the name of a line of low-fat dairy products back then. I didn't vote for that name. I thought we should have something more witty or clever, although I didn't offer anything zingy. Other names noted in the Camp Stanley brochure include Incredible Inches and Gourmets Gallery (sans possessive apostrophe).

One of the bunks housing counselors bore the name "Cuntry Club." The counselors were just being *méchant* (as we say in Quebec) iconoclasts, owning the epithet and assuming their charges didn't get the double entendre—except for the campers who had older brothers with *Lady Chatterley's Lover* hidden under the mattress, who may have encountered the word before and knew what it meant. I had one of those brothers.

The Division Four bunk was a long, barracks-like building, with beds on either side of a hallway that went to the back, arriving at the shared bathroom. There were about thirty girls in each bunk. Every two beds there was a plywood half-wall to provide a scintilla of faux privacy. It gave the impression there were two beds to a "room" and the occupants shared a sink with the two occupants of the next "room."

There was a window over each set of two beds. A two-shelf night table between the beds allowed each girl a cubby hole for storage. Each girl had a Camp Stanley calendar available to mark weight-loss milestones and scratch off days endured, like a "prisoner pent" in Shakespeare's sonnet.

* * *

Hungry pubescent girls in a group are dangerous.

For instance, my birthday that summer didn't offer a cake to celebrate. No, the Camp Stanley version was a red cabbage with a tealight candle on top. And yet you would have thought the raw, purple-y brassica vegetable I'd been given was a Lady Baltimore cake with fluffy buttercream icing, because everyone in my bunk wanted a cabbage leaf! I was mobbed, and within minutes, I was left with nothing but the central stalk and a bunch of bunkmates talking cake fantasies long after lights out. I stood in my pajamas, holding the denuded cabbage stalk, while a bunkmate took a picture. It was funny—except it wasn't.

Another food ritual was the weekly "canteen" day, where we got to spend the wee bit of the money parents had left for us to get stamps, stationery, film, toothpaste, tampons and—sugar-free candy. Food!

Some girls were candy bingers. The price you pay for candies sweetened by fake sugars such as sorbitol and saccharin can often be flatulence and loose bowels. Canteen day was often quite aromatic.

I've never been a big candy craver, so my MO to make the treats last was to spend my canteen money on sugar-free gum. Chewing a half-stick of gum helped suppress my appetite. I could also keep my mouth moist while exercising by thinking about biting into a lemon and chewing gum. I realize now the sensation I often thought of as hunger was, in fact, thirst from dehydration. Ditto fatigue. I often couldn't discern the difference between hungry and tired: at home, when I should have gone to bed, I made and ate a sandwich instead. Or cinnamon toast à la Dad: softened butter, cinnamon, and brown sugar spread on brown toast.

Other things we could buy on canteen days were tampons, sanitary napkins, and cocoa butter. The latter—delivered in small, yellow, metal tubes—was recommended by Gussie Mason and others as a treatment for stretch marks. Kids who grow up and fill out quickly during puberty can develop stretch marks. So do other adults who gain weight quickly: mothers, athletes, weightlifters. For young girls, it's usually on the abdomen, the hips, and the breasts.

I had a few silvery marks on my hips but nothing that concerned me. I bought the cocoa butter and massaged it in, but even seeing little change to a non-problem, I kept at it, mostly because of the fragrance. It's a wonderfully rich, creamy, chocolatey scent. And it's a great moisturizer.

Some of my fellow campers were quite alarmed by stretch marks. I saw a few girls in my bunk whose expansion had been so rapid that their stretch marks resembled angry, red lightning bolts on their hips and burgeoning young breasts. Applying cocoa butter was widely adopted as part of girls' bedtime ablutions. The bunk was usually redolent with the buttery fragrance after lights-out.

The scent was so evocative of times when girls could eat what and whenever they wanted, that I would often see bunkmates just sitting with their open tube of cocoa butter, inhaling the aroma as though it were a perfume tester. It was rumored some girls went further than sniffing and took an actual bite. Apparently you could tell who did this by noting how many tubes of cocoa butter a person bought on canteen day.

One tube of cocoa butter lasted me all summer. After becoming familiar with the texture on my fingertips, I was never tempted to try a taste. I still use cocoa butter as a moisturizer sometimes; just one whiff of that rich smell as I twist off the cap transports me back to Bunk L, Division Four, in Hurleyville, falling asleep surrounded by other thirteen-year-old fat girls tormented by stretch marks.

* * *

I was anxious about having a roommate, as I had already spent too long in too little square footage with my sister. I struck it lucky with the girl in the other bed. She was a real character, very funny, and with a big heart. She was from New York City; specifically Jamaica, Queen's. I had to have the NYC boroughs and neighborhoods explained to me: How could there be a place called Jamaica in New York City? She had long, thick, lilting dark hair and an easy, distinctive laugh.

While friendly enough, she initially hung back and observed. But when she had something to say, she said it clearly and loudly. As we got to know each other better, she became downright chatty. To a Canadian girl, having a roommate with a New York accent was like having a roommate from a US television show, the only place I would previously have heard that accent.

She was also quietly compassionate. There were times at the start of my fat-camp sojourn when I became teary. I had vowed no one would see this, so I did my best to only let the tears slide when I was alone in a toilet cubicle or in bed after lights-out. A couple of times they snuck up on me in daylight, usually late afternoon "rest" in the bunk with my face turned toward the plywood wall, choking me until I released an almost-silent sob. She was the only witness. "Miss your folks?" was all she said. As I nodded frantically so I didn't have to speak, she reached over and tapped the back of my hand. And that was it. We sat together on opposite twin beds, staring at the floor, until I settled down.

She had been to Camp Stanley at least once before; she'd gained back some of the weight but not all of it. She was not fat but not svelte either, and she was fine with returning to try again to get the job done. Mostly, she seemed to like hanging out with her camp friends and enjoying life in the little Catskills bubble. I was surprised to learn that other campers had returned as well. It seemed there was comfort in being okay among others who were chubby. My roommate knew the lay of the land and knew what happened next. It was invaluable to have her so nearby (in the next bed!) and comforting as she graciously shared info that helped allay my generalized anxiety about the place.

As a New Yorker, she seemed very sophisticated to me. She'd been to a taping of *The Dick Cavett Show* and offered to take me if I visited her after camp. We stayed in touch, corresponding for years, and while I did once visit her in New York City, we never went to a Cavett taping. Some relationships don't necessarily wither, but neither do they thrive much beyond the confines of the small garden plot where they started.

* * *

I made one friend who was tall and beautiful with smooth dark skin, with some intriguing childhood scars and an afro. She was an athlete, a bit husky but not fat. She knew how to do many athletic things I didn't; I put that down to having brothers and going to an American school. Besides softball, golf and tennis, she knew stupid team sports like crab soccer, actual soccer, and track events I'd only read about.

This friend rescued me the Saturday night we were "treated" to roller skating around the tennis court. We were given access to skates like they were bowling shoes, and most of the girls knew how to swoop around, forward, backward, stop easily. Not me.

Roller skates were something I'd only seen in movies. I managed to wrestle them on and, miraculously, stand up. I grabbed the chain-link fence and made some progress hand-over-hand, but didn't have enough confidence to let go and try to skate. She came and showed me how to keep my knees bent and glide without face-planting. I got the hang of it but never enough to really enjoy it.

This girl and I became very good friends that summer and beyond. Our friendship led to a job the next summer as an au pair near where she lived. Another big adventure I undertook to get away from home.

* * *

When I think about the intense intimacy of girlish friendships, I remember their safety and the diminished threat of violence, betrayal, and, later, pregnancy. These memories help me understand today's inclination toward gender fluidity because as much as I talked about guys I usually much preferred spending time with my girlfriends—talking about guys.

One girl in our bunk had been to Camp Stanley the previous summer and lost a lot of weight. She was lovely and slim, non-neurotic. I wager that she, like others who were thin returnees, was back because she felt comfortable, had some friends she wanted to see again, and thought she had a few final pounds to lose. She didn't. What she did have was very elastic skin. She had lost about 150 pounds, and while her skin wasn't hanging off her in drapes, she could pull her skin away from her rib cage from six to eight inches, and let it snap back.

Another girl in my bunk had a mane of wavy hair, parted in the middle. She was another one who didn't strike me as at all fat. She was tall, with an easy smile, and she attracted other campers like the Pied Piper—but she didn't seem to have a close coterie. When I hear Carole King's "It's Too Late," I hear this girl singing it at the top of her lungs. I never witnessed her being disruptive or misbehaving, but she was called aside more than once by the senior counselors. One day, we came back to Bunk L after lunch to find her packing; she was being picked up that afternoon. Her bunkmates cried and said they'd miss her as they hugged. I never found out what she did to get expelled (there were rumors of smoking), but I certainly envied her going home.

* * *

It was at Camp Stanley that I really learned I wasn't necessarily the genius I thought I was. I often thought my ideas were just the best, and went out of my way to make them manifest. Often I imposed them on others with extreme persuasion by my big personality. I was used to being called "bossy." Not my favorite descriptor; I preferred "smart." And "mature." And "funny."

"Moira can be domineering at times," my fifth-grade teacher wrote in my report card. I had to look it up and then ask my mother for help to understand it, although I knew it wasn't a compliment. Mum calmly explained it but told me years later how she nearly blew a gasket when she saw that word attached to a little girl. As I got older, I learned to bite my tongue, but it was always a struggle to see how long I could keep my mouth shut when confronted by a vacuum. Or the silence of indecision. Or the silence of not wanting to make the first move.

We had to do a "bunk" project in teams, some kind of carnival midway creation. I came up with a computer where people would pay to ask a question and "the computer" would come up with a response. We got a box big enough for two of us to sit inside. We punched symmetrical holes in it and covered those on the inside with different colored cellophane sheets. One of us then waved a camper's flashlight to create blinking lights, like the ones on the control panels of the Enterprise on *Star Trek*. Of course we got hot and cranky stuck in that box, and the lighting effect really failed in the middle of a sunny day. I also hadn't thought through the delivery of the answers: the questions came in written on index cards, but none of us could deliver a good computer-robot voice, so we tried scribbling our answers on the reverse of the cards the questions arrived on.

The trouble quickly became apparent: both questions and answers were illegible. And people were asking questions we couldn't answer. "Just make stuff up," I said confidently. "Make up *funny* stuff." But our answers were both wrong and unfunny. Oddly, the traffic to the computer dried up. My bunkmates glared and soon abandoned me to check out what the other bunks had done. Everything was better than ours apparently. I had to stay with the "computer" in case a camp counselor came to check.

* * *

The food at Camp Stanley was not memorable. I was often hungry in the short respite between exercise and meals, and I ate pretty much everything I was offered, except liver.

Help Your Child Lose Weight and Keep It Off included menus for 900-calorie and 1,500-calorie diets. There is also a seven-day, 1,200-calorie diet offered as a guide for creating individual meal plans in a family.

It's all so dispiritingly familiar.

Breakfast
Half banana, sliced
Two small Shredded Wheat biscuits
Glass of skim milk

Lunch
Beef stew (two ounces beef) with small onion, carrot, celery
Pickled beet salad dotted with egg yellows
Half-cup sherbet

Dinner
Clear chicken consommé
Fresh fruit platter: sliced fresh pineapple, half-cup fresh strawberries, half an orange, half a peach
Four tablespoons cottage cheese and one double Ry Krisp [rye cracker]
One glass powdered milk

Other tricky elements of these insufferable menus are the measurements; I always got into trouble when I started to believe I could eyeball or freehand a half-cup, or three tablespoons of whatever.

These kinds of menus are great if you have unlimited prep time and money for fresh fruit. On their own, most teenage dieters wouldn't immediately come up with "pickled beet salad dotted with egg yellows" (yolks).

When I was a power-dieting adolescent and young adult, I ate a lot of cottage cheese (which I quite liked, thank goodness), dill pickles, grapes (frozen, they're like little stickless, standalone Popsicles), apples, oranges, celery (the crunch that almost stops the yearning for potato chips), tuna, hard-boiled eggs, Melba toast, tasteless European crackers, coleslaw, sauerkraut—you get the picture. Vinegar, no mayonnaise. Protein boiled, grilled, roasted, not fried. Salads, minimalist: lettuce and lemon juice. Lots of water. Diet soft drinks, if they were handed to me; I never sought them out. Hated the taste, the fake sweetener coating the back of my tongue with the chalky feeling from chewing on Tums.

Hating diet soft drinks and low-fat treats probably saved me, in one way. I didn't become attached to any of it. I tried baking with sucralose (yuck) and reverted to just using less sugar. More fruit. I do like V8 juice and plain soda water, so I'm lucky.

Our regular drink at the long dining tables were jugs of what we called "bug juice." It must have been a low-cal, sweetened concoction made into a drink by adding water to powder. Even though we got skim-milk cocoa for breakfast, I missed my tea. Skim milk was an option at most meals, and Mason made the case for it in her book: "One of the welcome side-effects of serving milk may be a more emotionally stable teenager. A lack of calcium in the diet often causes many teenagers to become irritable and restless".

Contraband was rumored, although I never witnessed anything beyond a slice of angel-food cake wrapped in a napkin, dessert saved from a Sunday supper.

There was a tale of one camper whose brother had managed to smuggle her some real chocolate bars and a box of Life Savers on visitors' day. This was probably an apocryphal tale, but it did lead to the discussion among my bunkmates of an existential question: how many calories in a Wint-o-Green Life Saver? FYI: fifteen calories. And they're sweetened with sugar and corn syrup, the original sinners.

Saccharin was eventually revealed to be potentially carcinogenic in animals yet remains available. Sugar-free soft drinks sweetened with aspartame and/or sucralose may be just as bad for the consumer when it comes to raising blood sugar and increasing the appetite for sweetness. The search for a sugar-free sweetener continues, with stevia, a plant product, being one of the latest to be both studied by science and available to consumers.

Sweets and sweeteners were and continue to be a challenge for weight loss. Sugar-free was the dieting mantra for a long, long time. Then it changed to fat-free, until it became clear that to make something fat-free, sugar had to be added to provide flavor. (I'm looking at you, fat-free fruit-bottom yogurt.)

The calorie count of a small treat and its sweetening agent was the kind of existential question that pubescent girls in Camp Stanley's Bunk L, Division Four whispered about after lights-out, on those rare days when all the exercise they'd done hadn't left them so tired they blacked out before their heads hit the pillow.

CHAPTER 6

The scale or the guillotine: weekly weigh-in

"Tips for dieting insurance at home: 1) weigh your child each morning before breakfast and mark the weight on a calendar."
—*Gussie Mason*

The scale. And the calendar. Two more objects of tyranny. I had a calendar on the plywood half-wall that separated Gail and me from our two bunkmates.

I scratched a big X through each day as I counted off what felt like my imprisonment/abandonment. The calendar had a back page for your bunkmates' addresses and phone numbers; mine was filled before I left. That and my jacket, autographed by all my pals. I was always grateful for the friends I made.

Initially, it was a struggle to fall asleep in my single bed in Bunk L at Camp Stanley. I was lonely. I was frightened. I couldn't believe what was happening and I couldn't believe I had no recourse. Later on, because of the exercise, I was usually so tired I practically blacked out or "fell asleep before my head hit the pillow": that's how it's often described by those who may not want to consider how this level of exhaustion shows up in children, wanting to imply it's because of lots of childhood fun rather than too much activity or exercise.

I stared at the visual texture in the plywood wall, and at the quarter-round at the top of the half-wall. When I touched it, there was no comfort in the texture. I would hug my knees, or the spare blanket, or my pillow. I could sometimes hear distant music coming from older campers' bunks. I can conjure the trapped-in-Camp-Stanley feelings when I think of the 1971 music; the Carpenters' "Rainy Days and Mondays," or Carole King's "I Feel the Earth Move."

That trapped feeling of having no agency was unbearable. I had to swallow hard, regularly, to keep my eyes from watering. All I said to myself as I swallowed was: *Don't, don't, don't, don't...* If I cried, a weak spot would be exposed. The world would know I wasn't grown up, that I was still a little girl. Or worse, my tears wouldn't be noticed. Or would be simply ignored.

It would be years before I learned that if I just started doing something with what was in front of me, I would feel better. Be here now, etc. It would also take me years to discern the difference between not being noticed and being ignored.

I had no one to talk to about how I felt at Camp Stanley, not that I would ever have shared this with a stranger such as a camp counselor. At home, I had our family counselor, an amazing woman. I didn't necessarily trust her to keep things in confidence, but she listened. I also knew I could plant things with her to transmit to my parents. This was never overt, but her complicity was largely assured.

At camp, I would lie in bed at night and try to think of a way out. I didn't have the nerve or the resources to run away. Even if I did, it would be quite clear where I was "escaping" from, even if I could get to the nearby town of Hurleyville. I would have to hitchhike! A terrifying prospect. And was there even a train or bus station in Hurleyville? Even if there was, money would be required. As I thought it all through, I was foiled at every turn by being a thirteen-year-old Canadian girl at camp in the Catskills.

The scale or the guillotine: weekly weigh-in 61

Most of the counselors were overweight. Some only claimed to be. They were all only a few years older than the girls they were supervising. Most acted like big sisters or older cousins. For many, this was a summer job to help pay for university while getting a few pounds off. The counselors with a wicked streak were popular, the ones who sometimes let slip a swear word or snuck a cigarette out behind the counselors' cabin at night. Among campers, only those older than sixteen who had parental permission in writing were allowed to smoke. It being the seventies, the counselors had a prescribed smoking spot, and we knew there were harsh penalties for getting caught: expulsion and dismissal.

And we liked the independent thinkers, such as the counselor who ignored Gussie Mason's directive to wear our brassieres to bed and suggested we do the same. This young woman had long hair she wore in a ponytail, and acted as though she had lots of brothers. Nothing shy about her; she'd had to fight for her share of dessert growing up, I wagered. I would never have described her as fat, to me she looked like an athlete who maybe had eaten too many cheeseburgers. She was going to MIT and was tough, smart, realistic, and funny.

There was another counselor, a Southerner who was particularly kind. She played the ukulele and sang, telling us that while she might have a "big bee-hind" (she did), she had tiny hands that she couldn't get around the neck of a guitar. That's why she'd taken up ukulele. This was where my love/hate reaction to the Southern accent started. Initially, while I really liked and admired this woman, I didn't trust the effusive nature of a Southern mien; I felt it to be insincere. Probably the result of being a frozen-breath, fast-talking Canadian. And very judge-y.

The senior counselor who oversaw the Light 'n' Livelies in all circumstances was a delightful young woman, short brown hair and a paintbrush-flick spray of freckles. There was an early event at which we were supposed to introduce ourselves in song. This counselor chose a tune to which she wrote Camp Stanley lyrics: "We're Division Four no one can beat us, we're Division Four, we are the best." I recognized the melody; I'd heard it on the radio, a compelling, jaunty instrumental, a rarity on AM radio in those days. We played along, gamely singing our theme song at appropriate moments. It was a unifying chant.

Years later, I heard the song again on the radio, bopped along, then heard the DJ announce that it was by Henry Mancini and the title was… "Baby Elephant Walk."

That stopped me cold. Had it been a cruel inside joke, to get their youthful charges, their own baby elephants, to sing along to that tune? Hilarious. Or was it just a nice tune containing an irony that escaped everyone at the time? I chose to believe the latter.

* * *

At school, I often called my Mum to complain of stomach aches or headaches to get out of school. But telephone use was beyond prohibited at Camp Stanley. Parents were told to call the office if they had crucial information to relay to their daughters, but not to call expecting to talk in person. Otherwise there would have been a daily lineup of girls wanting to call home. Although my parents had been called when I ended up in the infirmary with the flu.

I didn't have the nerve to try and engineer a phone call to get out of camp the way I got out of school. I knew I probably wouldn't get the response I wanted; they would have to accept the collect charges and would have initially panicked. That's no way to persuade reluctant people to do what you wished.

I was left with daily letters. I wrote to my mother and father separately, begging desperately to be brought home, citing facts about the camp's decrepitude. I exaggerated some, as didn't really know how things were supposed to be at a place like Camp Stanley.

However, I did know that grass on a golf course should be sufficiently trimmed; I knew enough that you should be able to see a ball on the fairway. And I did know the pedals on a paddle boat were supposed to work.

But mostly my letters were sad, bad, purple-prose bleating about how lonesome I was, and how hungry. How tired and how scared. The message was sincere but hyperbolic. I thought the food was poison, or at least tasteless. The exercise was bloody torture, or at least cruel and unusual punishment.

While I received daily letters from my father, and less frequent missives from my mother, no letter from anyone directly responded to my pleas. I got news from Lachine, the parish, weather descriptions and forecasts in Montreal, what was new on display at Man and His World (previously Expo '67), the state of the shadfly swarm on Lake St. Louis, and how many golf balls my father had retrieved when he jogged through the Grovehill Golf Course.

I wonder now if my pleas had been less graphic, less caricatured, less pathetic, if I would have received a direct response. Although I never asked them why they had sent me away. *Really, why? I know you tell me you think it will make me feel better and deal with something I'd wrestled with for so long.*

I wish we'd had a phrase in the family lexicon that signaled: *I'm serious. I'm in trouble. Help me.*

Every day at camp, I woke a bit early. I always wished I could have slept a little longer to avoid the day I knew was coming. The same as the day before, I still had a feeling like a flat lump in my abdomen. A lump of fear. Or regret, or yearning for home, acceptance, something. I couldn't make it go away by going to the bathroom, by breathing, or massaging my tummy, or expanding my tummy out, the way you do when you're pretending to be Santa Claus.

I dreaded another day. I wondered and wondered: What had I done that my parents sent me away? What could I say or do to persuade them to take me back?

Then there was the particular torment of weekly weigh-in. It was Sunday morning, and it wasn't as public as it was in *A Matter of Fat*. In the film, the weigh-ins took place outside, with campers lined up near mechanical doctors' scales. Instead, we went behind a screen of sorts, with a camp "official" who manipulated the scale and noted the change in our files. My weight went down appreciably the first week and then almost not at all the next week; and then down again the third week. That's been my weight-loss pattern for much of my life.

Right after I met my husband, I thought I should lose some weight because I really liked this guy. I had felt plenty attractive and sweetly voluptuous as things got started. I tested the waters of acceptance with some self-deprecation, and he said, "You're fine. You just want to get a bit of exercise."

I succumbed to the lure of an ad for a weight clinic. I borrowed the money from my mother. In my interview, the counselor asked about my motivations and gave me a knowing smile after I admitted I had "met a guy." I had to go to the clinic every day, get weighed, take a supplement. No shots. I had to eat only five hundred calories a day. Hot water with lemon every morning. No alcohol. Testing my pee for ketones. Lots of steamed fish with lemon. Chicken bouillon with scallions or chives. Only black coffee, but along with black tea, it was discouraged because they could contribute to dehydration. This is when I gave up sugar in my tea forever.

I lost weight that first year of romance. Not much more exercise. I remember feeling dizzy sometimes. I couldn't stay on that regime of five hundred calories a day and so I started to add foods like veal piccata and Caesar salad, which felt high protein and low carb (if you picked out the croutons). I didn't think too much about high fat.

In the NFB film, Lorne Greene's narration talks about the class elements of obesity and thinness. It used to be the rich were fat because they could afford it and they didn't have to work. Now, similar to when the film was made, the poor are more likely to be obese.

The narration says it cost $1,000 to send a daughter to Camp Stanley for eight weeks. My mother used her bonds as collateral to get bank loans for various things. As I noted earlier, she described them as appearing "frayed" from having been removed and replaced in her safety-deposit box so often.

One of the times was to pay for Camp Stanley.

* * *

In the sixties and seventies, buying "army surplus" was all the rage. I bought a partitioned sturdy canvas bag and used it as a purse without realizing it had been a gas-mask carrier. I found it more curious than horrifying. I also had a jacket, perhaps inherited from my father. It was a tan-colored canvas with sturdy snaps and a flannel lining. It was water-resistant, meaning it took a while to feel soaked in the rain. I took it with me to fat camp and when I left, many of the girls signed it in ballpoint. I still have it.

I got things started by writing on the back on the shoulder plate just below the collar: *I went to Camp Stanley, so pity me...*

That was the opening line of a song we screeched regularly as a group, usually arms linked, walking from one place to another.

"I went to Camp Stanley, so pity me
There's not a boy in the vicinity
And every night at 9 they lock the doors
I don't know why the hell I ever came before
I'm going to pack my bags and homeward bound.
I'm going to turn this whole camp upside down"

The sentiments my fellow campers expressed on the jacket are consistent and melancholy, stiff with early teen sentimentality. "Loving." "Missing." The word "skinny" is used much too much, as that was what obsessed us. Most are signed with first name only, but even just a first name has the power to conjure up a face from long ago in front of my mind's eye.

CHAPTER 7

Adolescent cynicism: "If she mentions the goddamn edema in her leg one more time, I swear…"

"My secret weapon in the war on fat is the Beautiboot, which I invented and hold a US government patent on."
—*Gussie Mason*

The daily routine at Camp Stanley established itself quickly, built around meals and exercise. This had been clearly outlined in the brochure sent to my parents. I pored over that brochure before I got there, trying to imagine what was coming my way.

A typical Camp Stanley day
7:30 Reveille
7:45 Flag raising

8:00 Breakfast (Infirmary call after breakfast and after dinner)
9:15 A major sports activity (swimming, tennis or Slimnastics)
10:15 Minor activity (See list of minor activities)
11:15 Major activity #2
12:15 Prepare for lunch
12:30 Lunch

REST AND FREE TIME

2:00 Minor activity
3:00 Major activity #3
4:00 Rest / snack time
4:30 Minor activity
5:30 Prepare for dinner
6:00 Dinner

FREE TIME AND CANTEEN

8:00 Evening program
9:15 Taps juniors
9:30 Taps intermediates
10:30 Taps seniors
Before Taps, each group has a "night snack."

The minor activities listed in the brochure included golf, fencing, track, badminton, water bikes, baseball, archery, horseback riding, tetherball, volleyball, baton twirling, and field hockey.

At a handicraft workshop, we'd spend an hour making camp-standard things such as braided plastic friendship bracelets and dipped wire flowers. The latter was a popular craft at the time, creating flower- and leaf-shaped wire armatures that were then dipped in quick-drying plastic. It was quite stinky and gave me headaches. I wondered if anyone ever got high (glue sniffing was a thing, I knew) and I was glad for the open windows and airiness of the room.

The minor activities involved some things I knew I liked, such as badminton, and things I knew I hated: tetherball and volleyball, in which I always either got whacked or ended up with blood blisters and bruises all up and down my forearms.

I don't remember meeting a horse, because I would have enjoyed learning how to ride a horse.

In the Camp Stanley brochure, a girl was pictured in a silver mesh fencing mask against a bright blue sky, wearing the heavy canvas chest protector. She held her right arm curved up behind her head while wielding the foil in her left hand against an out-of-frame opponent. I was intrigued. I liked the ritual and the hand-eye coordination of fencing. I didn't like the shuddering legs I experienced after just twenty minutes maintaining some of the positions required, but my strength increased over the summer and the shuddering ceased. Some girls were scared they would develop "thunder thighs" from fencing, but that never concerned me. I appreciated the strength implied by muscled legs.

Archery was another sport I had never encountered but quite loved. Again, I liked the ritual and the history and the hand-eye coordination required. The archery counselor was wonderful, a petite blonde woman who I never would have considered fat. She was a good and patient teacher, with a head full of interesting, useful knowledge: I learned about bioflavonoids from her one day when we were all having our mid-afternoon snack of oranges. She knew all about orange-rind pith and how it was a good thing to eat because it contained bioflavonoids, even as so many campers said, "Ew! Yuck! Orange strings!" I still think of her and smile every time I peel an orange. She had been a champion archer, and shared her love of the sport with our gaggle of often-sullen teens.

Another draw of both fencing and archery was how sweaty I didn't get. Or how oafish and slow I didn't feel. These were both stand-and-think-and-concentrate activities, my favorite kind: no sweating involved.

And both were *armed* exercise. An exercise regime I could use some day to vanquish my enemies while imitating Zorro/Robin Hood/Thierry LaFronde.

The nine-hole-par-three golf course where I learned the basics was very ... basic. As was the well-intentioned instruction. The biggest problem was the speed at which the grass grew and how rarely it seemed to be cut. We young golfers often lost our balls in the fairway grass.

It quickly became clear who had learned some tricks from a golfing parent, and who had some experience playing with more than two irons. Lots of girls learned much from their golfing peers as soon as it was obvious who could play and who was deliberately driving their ball into the tall grass off the first tee, so they could spend the golfing hour goofing off and rooting around searching for a ball rather than actually trying to learn how to play.

* * *

There was another place the brochure called the "Fun Field," which was actually a kind of circuit-training course. Again, stuff I discovered I was good at—balance bars and fast, boxer-style skip rope—coupled with stuff I loathed: basketball, baseball.

I so wish I hadn't been turned off playing baseball when I was young. I remember one fun summer afternoon when I was about seven years old playing with visiting cousins of a neighbor in the shade of a weeping willow, playing with a fat plastic bat, running the path between improvised "bases"—including hats and lawn chair cushions—and laughing, laughing.

But between then and finding myself at Camp Stanley, praying the ball wouldn't come to me in the outfield while swatting at mosquitos, there had been no opportunity to develop any affection for the game.

Lots of girls there played softball back home, and many had skills that weren't undermined in the slightest by their heft. I was not a bad hitter: again, hand-eye coordination. But I kept getting into trouble for "throwing" the bat after I'd hit the ball. To my mind, it wasn't thrown as much as dropped quickly while proceeding to first base.

I kept being yelled at for this and ultimately slowing the game down. After that, I rarely had to endure the excruciating pecking-order process of team-choosing. I was the last.

There was a track for running: also not my fave; I try to run only when being chased by a bear or trying to get into a subway car. Some campers, the ones who weren't losing weight fast enough, would go there for extracurricular running, sometimes with dangerous results.

If a camper hit a weight-loss plateau, there was the option to try a short-term crash diet, somewhat similar to the 900-calorie diet in Mason's book. You could tell who was doing this because at breakfast, all they had on their tray was a plate with two hard boiled eggs and a two-Melba toast packet (the breakfasts in the book are more varied). Sometimes the caloric drop was enough to restart the process; if it didn't happen quickly enough, some girls upped their activity levels. You'd see them getting up early and running on the track before breakfast. Or when the schedule said they were supposed to be enjoying rest or free time.

There was one lovely girl in my division who wasn't at all fat. Her results weren't satisfying her, and she went on the lower-calorie, higher-activity-level regime to try and break the logjam. She jogged the track with such conviction and determination, increasingly red in the face even as her wrists and hands stayed properly relaxed and limp.

One day, as we were straggling back to the bunks to get ready for dinner, this girl continued to run the track and collapsed. After she was roused and given something to drink, she spent a few days in the infirmary. It was all very dramatic—and quite unhealthy. When we asked one of the counselors about this, she gave us a talk about dehydration and overdoing it.

My weight loss stalled, but I wasn't interested in more exercise and/or less food. It happened to many girls who were experiencing the natural result of increased exercise: increased muscle mass as they got stronger. Muscle weighs more than fat. I looked better and my clothes were looser, even if the change wasn't showing up on the scale.

* * *

The big three sports at Camp Stanley were tennis, swimming, and "Slimnastics."

My tennis game improved. With my mother's old racket, I had often played off the board in the park on my street. I played in my school uniform. It was solitary; I didn't know anyone else who played. At camp, I learned how to play murderous doubles. I wasn't bad, and was very competitive. These are two things I've long turned away from: confidence in my ability in most of any sphere where I apply myself, and my desire to win. I pretend I'm not competitive so I'm less invested in winning.

Swimming was great. I don't remember not knowing how to swim. For a chubby girl, the weightlessness is heaven. It's even worth the torture of swimsuit shopping. We had a variety of pool activities, many of which are now called aquafit. Sometimes we just had the opportunity to swim lengths. Languorous lengths, with no shouting from an instructor or coach. It was a chance to do an Esther Williams–style dive and use synchronized swimming skills to stay underwater, learned from TV and watching my sister.

Slimnastics was essentially calisthenics with light weights. Inspired by seeing figure skaters' great legs, shapely because they did everything with the weight of skates on their feet, Mason had patented the "Beautiboot"—a kind of two-pound beanbag affixed to your feet or held in your hands for extra resistance when lifting, bending, or squatting. These classes were mostly indoors and were fairly low key.

In her book, Mason includes a plan for homemade Beautiboots, saying, "I believe it is the best way to reduce legs and thighs and develop a good figure."

There are even diagrams for creating the Beautiboots: "All you need are four pounds of dried beans or peas, two yards of one-inch-wide ribbon or tape, and two eighteen-inch square measures of heavy cloth—towels or napkins will do." Explicit instructions follow on where to fold and sew, and how to "tie the Beautiboots on as you would sandals." Mason advises, "Always point your heels instead of your toes" and to "lift only one leg at a time."

At Camp Stanley, these exercises were conducted either outside on blankets or in a large interior space with a stage. Mason often led these classes herself. They sometimes ended with a little talk, usually about her own early struggles with weight and how she invented the Beautiboot. She talked about how Beautiboot exercises helped her recover from an injury. We sat cross-legged and listened, or lay down on the blankets and listened (I once snuck in a short nap). One day, as we filed in for the class, I heard a fellow camper say *sotto voce*: "If she mentions the goddamn edema in her leg one more time, I swear, I will lose it."

They may have been well-intentioned, but these little lectures felt like nagging.

In the film *A Matter of Fat*, Mason rails against nagging: "Just about every girl that came to me had the same experience: she was very pretty, very plump and all of her aunts and her uncles petted her and said, 'She'll outgrow it when she goes to school.' And then all of a sudden, the same people who petted her suddenly pulled the rug out from [under] her and everybody turns on her: 'You're too fat, and why don't you lose weight and you'd be so much prettier and why don't you, why don't you...' The poor child doesn't know what to do, what's hit her. Everybody that loved her [now] hates her, but nobody *really* hates her, they think they're helping her by nagging her. And that's what I tell them when they come to camp: There'll be no nagging whatsoever. Forget about it."

She rails about it in her book, even making it her number-one commandment. (I appreciate that Mason uses male/female pronouns interchangeably, so it's not just advice for the parents of fat girls.) "Thou shalt not nag. A child who wants to lose weight doesn't need to be reminded of his problem ten times a day. He'll control his eating habits to please himself. If he's not ready to begin a serious weight-control program, no amount of urging from his parents will help. The constant reminders of what he ought to do will just make it that much harder for him to do it when he's ready. He'll start to think of losing weight as showing weakness and "giving in." So don't let nagging turn weight control into a test of wills between you and your child."

The rest of her commandments go like this:

2. "Thou shalt not be sarcastic."

I had many things said to me about my weight both inside and outside the family, but I never experienced sarcasm. Mason says the motivating belief is "the child will lose weight just to escape being the butt of jokes." She adds: "An overweight child doesn't need any encouragement to feel unhappy. He feels worthless enough without his parents and family reminding him that people don't like him because he's fat. When parents join the chorus of criticism, the child's worst fears are confirmed. He believes that because he is fat, there is nobody in the whole world he can trust. This feeling of rejection is so awful that it saps the child's strength, and he begins to retreat into his own world. Instead of strengthening his will to diet, sarcasm destroys it."

3. "Thou shalt not put a price tag on your love."

I never felt as though there was a price tag, but I felt as though I couldn't come home until I was thin. A variation.

4. "Thou shalt not lock up the cookies and candies."

Nothing I experienced. Lots of things simply never made it into the house.

5. "Thou shalt not offer bribes."

Nothing I experienced. The closest I came was when my dad promised to paint my room while I was away at Camp Stanley.

6. "Thou shalt take your child into your confidence."

"A child understands more than we think," wrote Mason. "When the family faces a financial crisis, when one member is handicapped physically, or when a father or mother is drinking so much that he or she is getting close to alcoholism, the youngster is well aware of the situation."

I so wish my parents had known about this, considered it, and practiced it. It always felt as though things happened *to* me, not with me involved in the decision-making in any way. They often felt sprung on me. So much whispering, barely audible conversations behind closed bedroom doors until there was an ostentatious family conference. It felt modeled on something in *Family Circle* magazine or in a book about transactional analysis in the family.

7. "Thou shalt make weight control a family project."

This happened covertly sometimes, when Dad was dieting. The menu would change. More yogurt in the fridge. Skim milk. Saccharin packets or tablets in little blue tins would be in evidence. We'd have Hollywood-brand bread in the house (two slices had the calories of one regular slice).

8. "Thou shalt make home life as stable as possible."

Best efforts were made, but derailed by alcohol, mental illness, work, life circumstance.

9. "Thou shalt be a paragon of patience."

What might have been patience, as a sullen teenager, I read as indifference. Yet I suspect I would have been irate if anyone had butted in.

10. "Thou shalt be wrong... at least some of the time."

I wish my parents had later said: sorry about Camp Stanley. But they didn't. It was only under another guise that I later learned a truth—a truth that, had I known, I would probably have played along and worked Camp Stanley to my advantage.

CHAPTER 8

Visitors' day: please release me, redux

Many of us at Camp Stanley had the date for visitors' day circled on our wall calendars, the same place we marked off each day passed with an X, like pent-up prisoners.

About ten days before visitors' day we got instructions to start tidying up our cabins and environs. On a larger scale, I remember some of the buildings were spruced up, as well as some of the facilities, such as the tennis courts and the paddle boats. And they finally mowed the grass on the golf course.

The tall-grass had been high on the litany of woes I laid out to my parents as they took a tour of Camp Stanley: "This is the golf course. Can you believe it? You should have seen how long the grass was earlier this week! You could lose a ball right after your first shot, if you didn't keep an eagle eye on it. And your tennis shoes could get soaked in the grass wet from dew if you had golf first thing after breakfast. They cut it just before the parents got here, so it would look good."

We were encouraged to wear clothing that was more uniform-like on visitors' day. A light shirt and dark shorts, say. And clean! We had laundry done weekly, but teenaged girls weren't necessarily consistent about making sure everything was laundered every week.

I counted the sleeps until visitors' day, never wanting to exhibit my desperation to fellow campers. I knew I could persuasively make my case to go home. I even packed a small unobtrusive bag so I could leave with them, if things worked out perfectly. I hadn't calibrated realistically, because they hadn't driven from Montreal to Hurleyville, NY. (impossible for short visitors' window in a single day); instead, they flew and then rented a car.

My parents arrived with a surprise: the friend who had rescued me on fight night.

Seeing her brought me back to reality: she and my parents were there and then they wouldn't be there but I still would be.

Nonetheless I was so glad to see her, because I knew if I could get her alone, I could tell her the truth about what was going on and she'd believe me, about the non-mown grass on the golf course. And the stupid Cool Whip with an American flag stuck in it atop a chocolate pudding dessert to celebrate July 4. And getting a red cabbage with a candle in it for my birthday, and within an hour having nothing left but a stalk because the girls were so hungry that they all wanted a cabbage leaf. I felt so weird and out of place, so Canadian. I just wanted to go home.

It was so odd to "give them the tour" as they were all sort of dressed up, and I was in my clean camper clothes—but still, we're talking shorts and a T-shirt and running shoes. I had lost some weight, so there was much commentary on that. Admiration mixed with unspoken confirmation of their rightness in sending me there: "See? It's working." My father took pictures. My parents met my new friends.

And my friend from home—what an awful situation to put her in. I thought of the expense of that third plane ticket. What was my parents' thought process? Did they think I wouldn't make a scene because she was there? I wanted to cry the whole time because I knew I wasn't leaving that day. I knew my parents had on their rose-colored glasses and were seeing Camp Stanley in Technicolor while I was living it in B&W.

I did, however, claim a victory that day.

I pointed out to my parents that they were scheduled to be in Europe when camp ended—and how would I get home? This utterly terrified me, that I would be forgotten in the Catskills, with no way to get home. When I brought up the timing issue, I saw the look of dawning realization on my father's face and then my mother's. It landed as though this hadn't been considered before.

It was acknowledged, but specifics of my early departure were not clarified that day. By leaving Camp Stanley early, I was going to miss "color war" and being in the musical *Brigadoon*. I was going to miss the chance to buy new clothes for my less-fat body at the end-of-camp shopping trip. We were swapping clothes already as we dropped dress sizes, and I had my escape-from-Camp-Stanley outfit chosen already. It was a white shirt worn over the "Woodstock pants" I'd acquired from another Canadian there. She was there for her second year. Woodstock pants were low-slung bell bottoms made of denim with a Woodstock festival crowd scene printed on the fabric. I thought I was fair grand in this outfit.

I never really unpacked my duffel bag after visitors' day. I knew what day my dad was arriving to pick me up in our car but not what time. I said goodbye to my friends right after breakfast. I wore my hair down and waited where I could stay dry (it was a gray drizzly day) and see his car when it nosed into the Camp Stanley driveway.

When I spotted it, I felt such a whoosh of relief! I had the elevator-tummy sensation as I walked down the driveway toward him. I tried to stay cool and stride purposefully toward rescue, but soon I was trotting and then running.

My father took Super8 film of me running toward the car, in my Woodstock pants and my red-and-gray plaid raincoat. I'm glad there's a record of this pivotal moment.

CHAPTER 9

Rescued: it was the best day of my life

"You must ... begin to analyze your child's world in order to discover why he has put on so much weight."
—*Gussie Mason*

On the long drive home, I was finally able to exhale safely, completely. It was raining sporadically. My father picked up a couple of hitchhikers, two college-age guys. I was surprised, slightly alarmed, and then admired my father for giving these two a ride and how he chatted them up while making eye contact in the rear-view mirror and then knowing when to let things lapse into comfortable silence. It felt good when we crossed the border into Canada at night. I could hear *The Mikado* soundtrack being *whistled* and thinking my father had found the weirdest, hokiest FM station in the world. I was home before I realized it had been him, my father, who had most impressively whistled an entire Gilbert and Sullivan operetta while driving from the Catskills to Montreal, ferrying his desperate daughter home from an experience that changed her forever, but not necessarily in the way hoped for.

CHAPTER 9

Rescue: It was the best day of my life

CHAPTER 10

Weight loss today

What do we do, now that you can take a pill to lose weight, no need to diet or exercise? Is there something ethical, a morality to consider? I've had to wrestle with diet and exercise much of my life to stay at a reasonable weight and remain healthy. The cruel part of me says if I had to/have to do that kind of work, so should you or anyone else trying to reduce.

Yet I took Ozempic as part of my diabetes treatment and experienced easy weight loss with minimal side effects—up to a point. The dosage increases incrementally, and when I got to the clinical level, I got very sick and I couldn't leave it behind fast enough. Nausea, stomach pain, a return of colitis symptoms.

After a time, in consultation with my physician, I tried Ozempic again at a lower dose—no side effects. It allowed me to reduce another diabetes drug. So my weight is down, my blood sugar is down, and I'm doing well.

I don't like the idea of being drug dependent to keep the weight off and my blood sugar down, but *c'est la vie*.

I understood that Ozempic weight loss is usually gained back after you stop taking the drug. Mine stayed off, but I have changed my eating and exercise regime. I lost more weight with another diabetes drug. I also re-committed to food plan adherence with some accountability; I'm checking in with somebody and getting diabetes-specific counsel from a dietician. This will make it harder to say, "Just this once, life is short, it won't matter," before eating a bag of chips or making cinnamon raisin toast just before bed. I'm also recalibrating my exercise regime: more strength training.

When I told people I'm writing this book, I got a response completely different from what I anticipated. I heard stories of sadness and heart hunger and cruelty that shouldn't surprise me, but they do. I don't know why I thought things might have improved in the years since 1971. I hear stories about young girls being denied access to community-center sports teams because of their size, or being told they can't sign up for figure skating but should sign up for hockey.

Same old, same old.

I have felt as though my current success is about to be wrenched from my grasp at any moment, because it's not the result of hard work and time spent at the gym as though I were a competitor, and not just a person with a family and a job trying to stay healthy. It feels like a cop-out.

I think about how much time I have spent worrying about my weight. I know it's not as much time as others. Early in high school, I realized how much time I was spending on makeup. I would apply makeup in the morning, as much as I could get away with. Then at lunch, after walking home, I'd slurp my soup with some crackers, and wash my face with soap and water. I had started to shine at around 11 am and the makeup had started to slide off. I'd then re-apply all that makeup, including some thick, sticky, highly scented Yardley's Pot o' Gloss for my lips before walking the eight blocks back to school.

At some point it occurred to me how much time I was spending on this makeup thing and how I could use this time otherwise. I could read books! I could fantasize about romance! I could think about sex! I could plot revenge!

Sometimes, I would stop paying much attention at all to how much I ate or how much I weighed or how I looked. This would be fine until one day I couldn't get into my clothes—or I was surprised by a UTI because I'd been shoehorning myself into a too-small pair of jeans, lying down on the bed to do up the zipper and wearing a voluminous blouse to hide the muffin top. Or my blouse buttons would be straining across my bosom and I'd need to use a safety pin to make sure the placket lay flat and I didn't look like "a slattern," one of my mother's favorite descriptors, usually directed at me when she was into her cups.

Like many women, I had a fat wardrobe and a skinny wardrobe. I was often glad I hadn't thrown out or given away that pair of black pull-on corduroys with the elastic waistband, or its equivalent. At the other end of the continuum, I'd be asked: "Is that a new coat/jacket/skirt/blouse?" And I'd often say: *No, I was just too fat for it for several years but I hung on to it.* This would often lead to a chat about changing fashions and how what comes around, goes around. I had a chance to do some unconscious virtue-signaling, by being frank and self-deprecating when what I really wanted to do was tell everybody to leave me alone.

* * *

Now that there is medicine to help with weight loss, will that help obesity be better considered a disease rather than a moral failing, a "weakness?"

What if there's a hair-split, where only diet-and-exercise weight loss is considered legitimate? Will people who have successfully slimmed down using drugs hide their method?

Being thin currently signals wealth, as in being able to afford the drugs. Being thin used to signal wealth another way: the luxury of time to do the exercise and execute the menus.

A class element is apparent. This will probably get worse, as people lobby their insurance companies to pay for the pricey drugs.

What will women (and some men) do with all that time returned to them by weight-loss drugs, time they don't have to spend counting calories or reps? Will society find another way to scapegoat and undermine people of differing sizes? At different ages and stages?

* * *

There is no one answer to why it's so hard for teens to attain and maintain a suitable body size. But there are several lenses through which individual circumstances can be considered in formulating a plan, with family, health, school, puberty, and poverty among them.

There are useful programs that can be executed at home or delivered at school or in the community, and much research is still being done. The biggest takeaway here is that being overweight is no longer sold as a moral failing, but simply as a manageable chronic condition. But in some body-positive circles, intentional weight loss is considered "fatphobic."

A recent Dalhousie University survey of 10,000 Canadians reports 42.3 percent say they gained weight during the pandemic, between six and ten pounds.

"Weight is not a behavior. That's the critical thing we try to get across to people," says Dr. Sara Kirk, a professor of health promotion at Dalhousie University and scientific director of the university's Healthy Population Institute.

When I was growing up, I believed that my inability to maintain a body weight, one dictated by teen magazines, was simply my moral failing made manifest. I thought I was weak, lazy, and, some days, even stupid, unable to say no to salt-and-vinegar potato chips and Aero chocolate bars. This conscious and unconscious conclusion was reinforced by many things in popular culture both then and now.

The usual culprits in obesity are: too many calories, often from food that's not necessarily nutritious, and from sugar-laden drinks; not enough exercise, too much sedentary sloth and screen time; and genes, if the child comes from and lives amid an overweight-prone family.

Your body starts changing when you hit the foothills of puberty and then climb the mountains of adolescence before it plateaus in early adulthood. If it's a good plateau, it's one you try to maintain as adulthood rolls out. Girls might start padding out when their menses start. Male hormones often mean a voice change, facial hair, and a growth spurt.

Girls endure societal pressure, and their interest in sweaty activity, particularly competitive sport, often drops off. Even "feminine" ways of staying fit, such as dance, swimming, and gymnastics, see a drop in engagement when it gets to a competitive level, most likely in adolescence.

When it comes to food, adolescents are making more food choices outside the family, swayed by peers, advertising, and "influencers." Fewer adolescents bring their lunch to school. Even fewer order a side of carrot sticks with a bunless cheeseburger, washed down by ice water with a twist.

The US Centers for Disease Control and Prevention list poor sleep routines and some medications as contributing factors to obesity in children and teenagers. The World Health Organization (WHO) published a fact sheet in 2020 noting that, in 2016, more than 340 million children and adolescents between the ages of five and nineteen were overweight or obese. The WHO further noted that 38 *million children under the age of five* were overweight or obese in 2019.

Obesity in children is now rising in countries with low and middle incomes, when it used to be considered a problem limited to countries with high family incomes. The WHO says the number of overweight children under age five in Africa has increased by nearly 24 percent since the start of this century. And in 2019, almost half the obese or overweight children under five lived in Asia.

The WHO adds that "obesity is preventable."

Dr. Stasia Hadjiyannakis is a pediatric endocrinologist at the Children's Hospital of Eastern Ontario (CHEO). She is Medical Director of the Centre for Healthy Active Living, which works with children and their families with severe, complex obesity to develop and execute an individual patient-focused coordinated plan of care. I interviewed her for this book.

"Risk for obesity is largely dependent on genetic and biologic risk factors," she said. "Weight loss—and especially sustained weight loss—is very challenging due to strong neuroendocrine mechanisms that protect against this."

Dr. Hadjiyannakis points out that each individual has a body weight index (BMI) determined by genes and environment and "not everybody with a high BMI needs to lose weight." This position was reinforced by a recent *Canadian Medical Association Journal* article that notes a big body isn't necessarily unhealthy: the best weight "may not be an 'ideal' weight on the BMI scale."

A recent US study published in the US journal *Pediatrics* showed an alarming BMI increase in about 500,000 children between two and seventeen years of age attending the Children's Hospital of Philadelphia Care Network during one twelve-month period of the pandemic. Results show "on average, overall obesity prevalence increased from 13.7 percent to 15.4 percent."

The study showed that study participants who were lower income, black, Hispanic, and/or publicly insured had the most pronounced increase. The greatest increase (2.6 percent) was among children aged five to nine. These children need encouragement to know how to best feed themselves, help to prepare the food—and get off the couch.

The study cited in *Pediatrics* recommends finding activities that lead to more physical exertion, families connecting to nutritious meals offered in a community setting, and advocating for agricultural policies that promote health.

A person's *risk* for obesity is also determined by genes, and both genes and environment can leave your body "predisposed to exploit that risk," says Dr. Hadjiyannakis. A body can gain weight easily and, once it's there, neuroendocrinology tends toward "locking weight in," making it harder to both lose weight and sustain weight loss.

"Healthy bodies exist in a wide range of shapes and sizes," says Dr. Hadjiyannakis. "Our focus, when working with children, youth, and families, is on improving overall health and well-being. Optimization of lifestyle habits *will improve health*, while the impact on body weight is modest."

She notes that effects of restrictive dieting are usually short-lived, particularly if the restriction is abrupt and short term, such as a hospital stay or a fat-camp sojourn, such as mine at Camp Stanley. The body's survival mechanism responds appropriately to the diminution in weight with hormones that help make the body's use of energy more efficient. In the case of fat camps, exercise helps build muscle, which is heavier than fat and contributes to the body's efficiency in nutrient use. This "metabolic adaptation" makes it harder to lose, or even sustain weight loss, and might even lead to *weight gain*. That's because these adaptations evolved during periods of food scarcity, when our ancestors fattened up when there was lots of food so they'd suffer less when there was a climate disaster or a war or a crop failure and food was hard to find.

Explanations of why you're *gaining* weight aren't much help—even when those explanations prove your body's genius in helping you avert death by starvation—when it feels as though you've just put a great deal of effort into *losing* weight.

Weight gain under any circumstance can have a severe negative effect on a young person's self-esteem. It can lead to increased social anxiety. It can then trigger coping mechanisms, such as extreme introversion, avoiding anything where one might encounter other people, including group activities such as team sports, aerobics classes, and other forms of exercise—and overeating, the result of which is what's causing the social anxiety.

At the other end of the continuum, coping mechanisms can include disordered eating: the Academy of Nutrition and Dietetics in the US says this could include frequent dieting, meal skipping, specific food anxieties, chronic weight fluctuations, compulsive eating habits, or rigid routines around food and exercise. Also eating disorders such as anorexia nervosa and bulimia.

It's heartbreaking to read the obituary of a relatively young person, usually a woman, who died because of the long-term effects of an eating disorder. Being obese can lead to diabetes and heart attacks; anorexia and bulimia can lead to heart problems and others, as well.

I flirted with the edges of bulimia when I was in high school. There were whispers, rumors that you could chew your food and spit it out without swallowing, getting nutrition but no calories. And if you swallowed by accident, you could make yourself throw up.

What? Puke by choice?

I didn't like to vomit and did my best to avoid it at all costs, so it appeared this wasn't for me. Still, like all humans looking for an easy out, I tried once—and failed. I couldn't get past making myself gag, tear up, and get sweaty. And that was that. The chew-and-spit whisper campaign of the seventies was fairly easy to ignore; it was mild compared to websites advocating the extremes of bulimia and anorexia.

I once lived with a roommate who was probably anorexic. She was very pretty and far too thin, focused on strange food predilections, an exercise obsession, and prone to volatile mood swings.

I was, later in a professional position, to ask a self-described "recovered anorexic" about the challenges of moving away from the harmful behaviors.

Nothing is scarier than a middle-aged anorexic, she said. When you're younger, after about two weeks of bingeing and purging, your brain isn't getting enough nutrition to help you think your way out of the mess you're in.

I chose too much food as my style of "disordered eating" over not enough. Neither is healthy.

The COVID-19 lockdowns led to both an obesity bomb and exacerbated difficulties treating young people with eating disorders of any type. Recent media reports show teens struggled with the effects of "isolation, a lack of routine, a loss of extracurricular activities, and negative social media influences."

Dr. Geoff Ball, a professor in the pediatric department at the University of Alberta in Edmonton and a Founding Director of the Pediatric Centre for Weight and Health, says societal factors are everywhere: potent, pervasive and undermining, particularly exposure to food marketing online. I interviewed Dr. Ball for this book.

He says kids are bombarded with negative messages "anytime they're on social media." Even though we're now more aware of the messages, it "doesn't mean we know how to tailor them to optimal effect." Or know how to effectively countermand them.

Dr. Ball says the environment for children at that transitional age is one of "social comparison," and it's a time when these comparisons become more meaningful. "The environment is not supportive of making healthy choices."

Dr. Ball says the biggest change is one of emphasis: there's "much less of an emphasis on weight and much more of an emphasis on health."

It used to be said not that you suffer from obesity but that "you are obese." At the other end of the spectrum the message is, "I'm big and I'm proud." The latter individuals don't see weight as a health issue at all: "It's just a [body's] feature, like height or shoe size." But Dr. Ball says he sees the young people dealing with "the challenges of life in a big body and how that's a really difficult thing in our society."

The stigma is profound, but Dr. Ball is encouraged by the recent changes wrought in changing bias and stigma in mental health. He thinks attitudes toward obesity and weight management are on a similar trajectory, but it's taking more time. The challenge, says Dr. Ball, is to encourage a nuanced, health-focused approach to childhood obesity.

* * *

While certain elements such as healthy food choices and prioritized exercise can be orchestrated by individuals, families, and social structures such as schools, Dr. Ball notes a unique and uncontrollable feature contributing to adolescent obesity risk: puberty.

While puberty can offer a welcome growth spurt that might help distribute body fat more evenly, the hormonal changes remain profound. While many of puberty's effects are transient, Dr. Ball notes research shows there can be longer-term impacts. Resistance to insulin changes; for example, obese kids may already experience insulin resistance from the excess weight, and puberty can make insulin resistance drop still further.

"It's one of those periods of time where the impact has historically been transient, like pregnancy," says Dr. Ball. "But we've learned there are longer-term impacts." Such as the potential for continued insulin resistance.

What can be done to help young people enduring the changes of puberty and battling societal pressures?

Dr. Ball says the goal is to help kids be happy and healthy. "The challenge is [that] society values a certain size," he adds. He says it's wise for parents to be aware of their kids' online influencers, and to talk about their messages, and reinforcing the positive ones.

It's also useful to be aware of situations where peer support programming can be utilized. "It's more impactful when they learn from each other," says Dr. Ball.

One notable example is that of the APPLE Schools in Alberta; APPLE stands for "A Project Promoting Healthy Living for Everyone." It started with a single donation in 2006 to help improve the health of Albertan schoolchildren. It now serves 21,000 students across Western Canada, "by improving their healthy eating, physical activity, and mental health habits."

APPLE Schools serve numerous communities with large Indigenous, Métis, and Inuit populations, among whom obesity and Type 2 diabetes risks are higher than in the general population.

Dr. Ball notes "there is no quick fix" when it comes to formulating programs to help combat obesity specifically in Indigenous communities, and health educators must be "open, flexible, and responsive."

"Every community is unique," he says, "and adds another level of complexity."

At a macro level, Dr. Ball notes, poverty is a major determining factor for childhood obesity.

"People with the fewest options need the most support," he says. "Time, choice, money [are all] limited, so food choices and activity can be compromised."

Epilogue: Carry that weight

"Thou shalt take your child into your confidence. A child understands more than we think. When the family faces a financial crisis, when one member is handicapped physically, or when a father or mother is drinking so much that he or she is getting close to alcoholism, the youngster is well aware of the situation."
—Gussie Mason

When I got home from Camp Stanley, I weighed 157 pounds: about 12 pounds lighter than when I'd left. I did some unhealthy things to keep those pounds off and lose a few more. Looking at my sister's beauty magazines and 25-cent Dell Purse Books, I believed I should weigh between 125 and 130 pounds, even though I'd grown to five foot eight. The best I could do was to weigh 147 pounds after I'd had the flu. For years I joked that "I weighed 147 pounds for about 20 minutes in 1972." Ha, ha.

I ate a lot of sauerkraut and bratwurst with mustard. Drank cans of Tab. I ate minimal toast. Consumed many juicy, summer tomatoes, quartered and eaten with salt over the kitchen sink, until the corners of my mouth cracked.

I tried Ayds, little wax-paper wrapped "chocolates" laden with appetite suppressants. These were readily available until AIDS made the product name unusable. I tried Metrecal, a liquid meal that came in cans.

I didn't seek it out, but I did get some speed from a classmate at school, who had a biker boyfriend. Diet pills. Pink, that were three-quarters square on the bottom and like a pointed roof on the top.

This was my short period of drug experimentation, buying hash oil and orange-barrel acid and speed. I once did several uppers after an appointment with our family counselor, and then talked my head off at Murray's restaurant, so much that my mother mentioned how chatty I was. I still managed to eat my favorite thing on the Murray's menu, steamed fruit pudding with white sauce. I doubt it was low cal.

So here I am, in deep middle age (my mid-sixties) and I weigh 145 pounds, just under the weight I used to joke about. I lost about 12 pounds at Camp Stanley. Yes, 12 pounds is the sum total of the weight I lost during those difficult weeks in the summer of 1971.

What I learned later was that Camp Stanley had been the idea of our family counselor, to get me away from my mother's incipient alcoholism and my parents' marriage challenges—and help me shed a few pounds while I was staying sane. She had found the ad in the *New York Times Magazine*.

If I'd known that, if I'd been invited in to the conspiracy, I might have been a better camper, not spending all my energy plotting my escape while chafing at constraints, real and imagined. For so long I felt that if I didn't stay below a certain poundage, I could again be banished. I got married after my husband-to-be made his proposal contingent on "agreed-upon conditions." His motives were pure; it was to give me a deadline, a framework for achieving a weight-loss goal. But I should have walked away: not from getting married, but from the time-frame deal. If I had done that, perhaps I wouldn't have felt, as I still do, that I have to work hard to be lovable. Be smarter. Work harder.

This is all dime-store psychoanalysis, but I want to reinforce how much I agree with Gussie Mason on this. Don't try for the blackmail makeover, or buying off your lovable fat child with a spa slimming vacation. Tell your child you love them forever, unconditionally and always, no matter what. And then you can offer help, if your child asks.

Do it their way. And you'll ultimately get your way, without losing the respect and trust of your child.

Acknowledgments

To the memory of my parents, Norm and Gerry Dann, who loved me very much and did the very best they could with the information available.

Thanks to my friend and agent, Rob Firing, for the terrific insight and great counsel.

Thanks to Ken Whyte of Sutherland House Books for seeing the potential and refining the story's focus.

Thanks to the creative nonfiction Master of Fine Arts program at University of King's College, Halifax, for the schooling and the friends.

Thanks to my friends at the Piggy and Paisley Tea Room for support and sustenance.

Love and gratitude, always, to my dear husband, Sam Bufalini.

Notes

Chapter 1

Gussie Mason, *Help Your Child Lose Weight and Keep It Off* (New York: Grosset & Dunlap, 1975).

A Matter of Fat. Directed by William Weintraub. National Film Board of Canada, 1969. https://collection.nfb.ca/film/matter_of_fat.

"Could Fining Parents Cut Childhood Obesity?" *BBC News*, February 12, 2015. https://www.bbc.com/news/magazine-31417102.

Buzz Aldrin, interview by Conan O'Brien, *Late Night with Conan O'Brien*, May 17, 2000.

Chapter 3

Camp Stanley brochure.

Chapter 4

Montreal Gazette, "Entertainment Life," May 17, 2019. https://www.montrealgazette.com/entertainment-life/article403347.html.

Chapter 5

Mason, *Help Your Child Lose Weight and Keep It Off*.

"Life Savers Wint O Green Mints Bag 6.25 oz," accessed March 10, 2025, https://www.life-savers.com/products/life-savers-wint-o-green-mints-bag-625-oz-life-savers-mints.

Chapter 6

Camp Stanley brochure.
Mason, *Help Your Child Lose Weight and Keep It Off.*
A Matter of Fat, directed by Weintraub.

Chapter 7

A Matter of Fat, directed by Weintraub.

Chapter 10

Centers for Disease Control and Prevention. "Childhood Obesity Facts," April 2, 2024. https://www.cdc.gov/obesity/childhood-obesity-facts/childhood-obesity-facts.html.
"Obesity in Children." UCSF Benioff Children's Hospitals [Publication date not available]. https://www.ucsfbenioffchildrens.org/conditions/obesity.
Agri-Food Analytics Lab, Dalhousie University. "COVID-19 Well Being," April 27, 2021. https://www.dal.ca/sites/agri-food/research/covid-19-well-being.html.
"Experts Say Focus on Behaviour, Not a Scale, as New Study Warns of Pandemic Youth Weight Gain." *CTV News Atlantic* [Publication date not available]. https://www.ctvnews.ca/atlantic/article/experts-say-focus-on-behaviour-not-a-scale-as-new-study-warns-of-pandemic-youth-weight-gain/.
APPLE Schools. "Our 2024 Impact Report is Here!" November 21, 2024. https://appleschools.ca.

Epilogue

Mason, *Help Your Child Lose Weight and Keep It Off.*